Lifescripts

Also by Stephen M. Pollan and Mark Levine

Live Rich

Die Broke

Lifescripts for Managers

Lifescripts for the Self-Employed

Lifescripts: What to Say to Get What You Want in 101 of Life's Toughest Situations

Surviving the Squeeze

The Total Negotiator

The Big Fix-Up: Renovating Your Home Without Losing Your Shirt

The Business of Living

Your Recession Handbook: How to Thrive and Profit During Hard Times

The Field Guide to Starting a Business

The Field Guide to Home Buying in America

Lifescripts

for Employees

Introduction by Stephen M. Pollan

Written by:

Mark Levine, Michael Caplan, Jonathon Epps,
Andrew Frothingham, Erik Kolbell, Deirdre Martin,
William Martin, Nick Morrow, Allison Noel,
Aldo Pascarella, and Roni Beth Tower

Macmillan • USA

MACMILLAN
A Pearson Education Macmillan Company
1633 Broadway
New York, NY 10019-6785

Macmillan Publishing books may be purchased for business or sales promotional use.
For information please write: Special Markets Department, Macmillan Publishing USA,
1633 Broadway, New York, NY 10019.

Book Design by Nick Anderson

Library of Congress Cataloging-in-Publication Data

Lifescripts for employees / introduction by Stephen M. Pollan; written by
    Mark Levine . . . [et al.].
        p.   cm.
    Includes index.
    ISBN 0-02-862623-0
      1. Business communication. 2. Interpersonal communication.
    3. Managing your boss.   I. Levine, Mark, 1958–

    HF5718.L516 1999
    650.1'3—dc21
                                                          98-55974
                                                             CIP

                        ISBN 0-02-862623-0

        Manufactured in the United States of America
            10 9 8 7 6 5 4 3 2 1

CONTENTS

CONTENTS

I'm the first to admit I don't know everything. I'm always turning to others to fill gaps in my own expertise. So when I was asked to put together this follow-up to *Lifescripts*, I knew that to dig deeper into the world of workplace communications and come back with original, creative, and pragmatic new material I'd need help. In response, I was lucky enough to be able to put together a team of outstanding lifescript authors, with their own unique qualifications, expertise, and approach.

Mark Levine is a writer and editor who has collaborated with Stephen Pollan on fourteen books, including the original *Lifescripts* and their recent best-selling contrarian looks at spending and earning money, *Die Broke* (HarperCollins, 1997) and *Live Rich* (HarperCollins, 1998). His work has also appeared in a variety of publications including *Worth, New York, Money,* and *Working Woman.* He has taught magazine writing at Cornell University and lectured at the Newhouse School at Syracuse University, and his articles have twice been nominated for National Magazine Awards. He lives in Ithaca, New York.

Michael Caplan is a freelance writer who lives in Manhattan. He is currently working in script development with Borracho Pictures.

Jonathon Epps is a sales and marketing consultant. He is the owner of The Selling Source, Inc., a consulting firm specializing in architectural specification sales and marketing and professional development. He lives in Ithaca, New York, with his wife, JoAnn Cornish-Epps, and their two children, Paula and Sam.

Andrew Frothingham is a Manhattan-based consultant and freelance writer specializing in business communications, including speeches, newsletters, training films, and inspirational T-shirts. He has written, cowritten, and ghost-written numerous reference and humor books, including *How to Make Use of a Useless Degree.* He became a full-time writer after careers as a teacher, researcher, advertising executive, and high-tech marketer. He earned two degrees from Harvard, and is now in the process of being reeducated by his young son.

Erik Kolbell is a graduate of Brown University, Yale Divinity School, and the University of Michigan. An ordained Congregational minister, Kolbell has served in university and church settings. He is also a licensed psychotherapist practicing in Manhattan. He has written articles for numerous publications, including *Newsweek, The New York Times, Parents,* and *Child.*

Deirdre Martin is a full-time freelance writer and member of both the American Society of Journalists and Authors and the Writer's Guild of America. Her work has appeared in a wide variety of publications, including *New Woman, McCall's, Seventeen, YM, Fitness, Bride's, Modern Maturity,* and *InsideSports.* She is the author of *The Real Life Guide to Investing for Retirement* (Avon 1998) and has written for the daytime drama *One Life to Live.*

William Martin spent more than three decades as a high school teacher and associate principal, having dialogues with students, teachers, administrators, building staff, and parents. He is now a freelance writer and educational consultant. He lives with his wife, Barbara, in Northport, New York.

Nick Morrow is a tax accountant practicing with Martin Geller CPA in Manhattan, and specializes in advising individual and small business clients on a range of tax issues, as well as personal and business matters. He has written articles for numerous publications and lectured before a wide variety of professional organizations. He was a contributing author to *How to Beat the System* (Rodale 1997).

Allison Noel is a freelance writer who specializes in parent-child communications. She is now applying that expertise personally for the first time. She lives with her husband, Jay, in Salem, Massachusetts.

Aldo Pascarella is an award-winning screenwriter, with film projects in development at SABAN Entertainment and Brad Krevoy's newly formed production company. A graduate of Dartmouth College and the University of Southern California's Cinema-Television School, he lives in Manhattan.

Roni Beth Tower, a clinical psychologist with a doctorate from Yale University, specializes in issues of work and relationships. A fellow of the Academy of Clinical Psychology and past president of the American Association for the Study of Mental Imagery, she counsels adolescents, adults, and couples at her Westport, Connecticut, practice.

The Magic of Lifescripts

I've been giving advice to people for most of my adult life. Usually, it's in my capacity as an attorney and financial advisor; but at other times it's as a son, husband, father, or friend. Most often I'm being asked for help with vital legal and financial matters; but sometimes I'm asked how to persuade a husband to lose weight or how to borrow money from a parent.

I suppose I've become a source of advice on these diverse areas because of my long and varied experience in the law and business; my reputation as an effective negotiator; my notoriety as an author and television commentator; and my unique personal brand of service and attention I offer clients, readers, and viewers.

I like to take people by the hand and lead them through a process, helping them plan and preparing them for potential obstacles. I try to break every project down into manageable steps. But despite my best efforts and explaining and coaching, there's always one last question: "But what do I *say*?" It doesn't matter if I'm helping a young couple buy their first home, an experienced corporate executive negotiate an employment contract, or my father complain to his insurance company. People always want to know which words they should use and how they should deal with possible responses.

To ease their anxiety, I tell the person to telephone me before the event so we can create a "lifescript" for the whole conversation: an outline of the entire conversation including counters, responses, and rejoinders. Usually the lifescript is used verbatim, but sometimes it simply serves as the extra measure of confidence the person needs to face a difficult, unpleasant, or awkward situation. Many of my clients are amazed at how effective these lifescripts can be, and how much better they fare using them.

I'd like to take total credit for the incredible efficacy of my lifescripts, but while my negotiating savvy and experiences do play a part, what really makes them work is that they're comprehensive plans for situations we usually don't plan for.

When Generals Powell and Schwarzkopf were ordered to attack the Iraqi forces occupying Kuwait, they didn't just wing it. They and their staffs sat down and planned for every eventuality. By the time they launched Operation Desert Storm, there was nothing that could surprise them. From the first moment to the last they were in charge, dictating the action. They were proactive, not reactive. Saddam Hussein and the Republican Guards didn't know what hit them.

Don't get me wrong. I'm not implying that life is a war—though we all have to deal with our share of petty tyrants and despots. What I'm saying is that if we plan out our interpersonal exchanges—whether they involve work, business, or our family lives—not only will they be easier to deal with but, more often than not, they'll turn out the way we want. With a lifescript, either directly in front of you or just in your head, you'll never be surprised. You'll have a plan that leads inexorably to your goal, regardless of which obstacle is thrown in your way. You'll have an answer to every question, a comeback to every crack, and a defense for every attack.

HOW TO USE LIFESCRIPTS

The following pages offer solutions for what are arguably forty-one of the most perplexing and problematic dialogues an employee will ever face.

Each lifescript begins with a general discussion of the overall *strategy* you should use in the dialogue, usually highlighting what your goal should be. Then the text briefly describes the *attitude* you should adopt—for example, righteous indignation or contrition. The entry then touches on what kinds of *preparation* you need before using the script—perhaps some research or the drafting of a memo. Next, are tips on *timing*—whether it's better to have this conversation Monday morning or Friday afternoon, for instance. Then, the text explains what your *behavior* should be like. This could involve body language or where you hold the conversation.

On the next page is the lifescript itself in flow-chart form. Most offer icebreakers, pitches, possible responses, counters, and retorts. Obviously, each lifescript is different because each conversation takes a different form.

After the flow chart some ideas for *adaptations* are offered—other situations when, with some minor modifications, you could use the same lifescript. Finally, they provide a few *key points* for each lifescript listed. You can use these as crib notes to bring with you to the dialogue.

These lifescripts can be used verbatim. The words have been chosen very carefully. However, I think it's best if you take the words offered and play around with them until they sound like your own. That's because everyone has different diction and sentence structure. There's nothing wrong with sounding prepared, as long as you sound like yourself.

With forty-one scripts and possible adaptations more than doubling that number, I think this book offers help in nearly every common workplace situation. However, I'm sure there are important situations I've left out, either because the authors and I simply didn't think of them, or because they're unique to you and the circumstances of your life.

Rather than require you to call me on the telephone to help you prepare a personal script, I thought I'd give you a brief course in the five rules behind these lifescripts. That way you'll be able to draft your own. (Though of course, you are welcome to call me if you get in a real pickle.) These are, in fact, the same rules the authors of these lifescripts followed.

Rule #1: Take Control of the Situation

If you gain nothing else from this book, let it be an understanding of this rule. The single most important element in getting these conversations to turn out the way you want is to take control of them. That doesn't mean you monopolize conversation or bully the other person. It simply means that, through your choice of words and reactions, you frame and steer it in the direction you want it to go.

In many cases, that means you make the first move, and by so doing, force the other person to respond. In other situations, it means responding in such a way that the other person is forced into retorts that you've already prepared to address. Unlike most *icebreakers*, these aren't written just to make the person delivering them more comfortable. They're written to force the other party into a position with a limited number of options. That way we can prepare responses to each of those limited options.

Rule #2: Say What You Want

I'm continually amazed at the inability of most people to come out and say exactly what they want. Whether it's because we don't want to be viewed as demanding or we're afraid of being turned down, most of us beat around the bush, imply, and drop hints rather than coming right out and saying what's on our mind.

In almost every lifescript there's a *pitch*: a direct, specific request. You can't rely on other people to infer what you're after or to pick up on your hints. And besides, if you don't come right out and ask directly, you're giving the other party a chance to sidestep the whole issue. Make them respond directly. It's easier to deal with an outright rejection than you might imagine.

Rule #3: Show Your Power Before You Use It

Subtle demonstrations of power are often just as effective as the outright use of that power. For instance, if you're a restaurant patron, you have two powers: your ability to make a scene and your willingness to pay your bill. By calling over a waiter or maitre d' and whispering that you're unhappy with your meal and would like another, you demonstrate that you're aware of your power to make a scene, but are holding it in check until they've had a chance to respond. If you actually raise your voice and make a scene immediately, you have far less power, since you've used up all your ammunition.

Other ways of displaying your power include saying things like "I'm a long-time customer and would like to continue our relationship," or "The last thing I want to do is hire someone else to finish this project." In both cases, you're showing an awareness of your power, but also a willingness not to use it. That's far more likely to work than an outright threat. Though if push comes to shove, you may have to make such a threat.

Rule #4: Absorb or Deflect Anger

That doesn't mean you should get angry, however. Displays of anger are just as self-defeating as gratuitous exercises of power. The actual message you send when you get angry is "I've no real power, so all I can do is make noise." Therefore, hold your temper whenever possible.

Similarly, when you're met with anger, the best response is to disarm the other party by either absorbing or deflecting it. You absorb anger by acknowledging it and refusing to respond in kind. ("I can understand your being angry. I would be, too.") You deflect anger by suggesting that it's an odd reaction and must, therefore, be based on something other than your request. ("I don't understand why you're getting angry at me. Have I done something else to bother you?")

Rule #5: Have the Last Word

In almost every situation, it's to your advantage to have the last word in a dialogue. That means either expressing thanks for getting what you wanted, asking for reconsideration of a rejection, or pushing for another meeting or saying that you'll call back if you couldn't get a definite answer. Having the last word does two things: It makes sure you retain the control over the dialogue that you seized when you broke the ice; and it allows you to close the conversation on advantageous terms.

The only exceptions to having the last word are in situations when it's important for you to give the other party a chance to "save face." In effect, by giving him the last word, you're letting him think he's still in control, even though he's not.

TWO PHILOSOPHICAL THOUGHTS

Before you jump into the lifescripts themselves, I need to touch on two important philosophical issues: the ethics of scripting conversations in advance, and the question of whether or not you use "white lies" to your advantage.

Some of the people I've helped develop lifescripts have voiced concerns about the ethics of scripting some dialogues. They feel workplace communication is more "honest" when it's spontaneous. Personally, I don't see anything wrong with preparing for office discussions, even informal ones. In fact, I think it's an excellent idea.

Sure, one of the major reasons people like my lifescripts is that they work. By using them, my clients have been able to get what they want out of life. But that's not the only advantage to lifescripts. When you plan a conversation out to this extent, you avoid a lot of the ancillary problems of human interaction. By scripting you avoid getting sidetracked into a discussion of why you didn't attend an employee's wedding, or why no one from your department participated in the Labor Day Walkathon. Granted, those may be two valid topics for discussion. But they should be topics in and of themselves, not background noise in a dialogue about office gossiping or potential vendor problems. By scripting you insure that the conversation will stay on track and in the process, avoid falling into argumentative patterns. I think that, far from being unfair or unethical, lifescripts help pave the way for smoother workplace relations and better office communications.

Finally, let's look at the issue of white lies. In a few of the lifescripts you'll notice lines such as, "I've already notified the boss about this," which effectively disarms threats from the other party. The authors are assuming that you're actually going to do what the lifescript says, in this case, speak to your boss before the meeting. Of course, that doesn't mean you have to in order to use the line. That's something you'll have to decide for yourself. But if I can offer one more word of advice in parting, it's this: The most effective lifescripts are truthful.

Stephen M. Pollan

I

Lifescripts

...for Your Boss

Meeting with a New Boss

1.

STRATEGY

Your first meeting with a new supervisor is vital, since it often sets the tone for the entire relationship. Whether your new boss is coming in to clean up a troubled situation or to step into the shoes of a successful manager who has moved on, and whether he is coming from within or without the company, you can count on one thing: He will want to put his own stamp on operations. That's why your goal in this first meeting should be to get a hint about his plans. In order to do that, make your first conversation seem spontaneous and casual—a simple welcome. Use whatever information you gain in this quick scouting mission to develop a full-fledged plan for a subsequent, in-depth, formal meeting.

TACTICS

- **Attitude:** Keep in mind this is only a scouting mission, but you still want to make a good first impression.
- **Preparation:** Learn as much as you can about your new boss's habits and history. Any specifics you learn can be used to make your subtle flattery more effective. Don't be concerned about actually using all your research.
- **Timing:** Timing is probably the key to pulling off this dialogue as planned. You must make sure to beat your new boss's secretary or assistant into the office, so you can casually just stick your head in the door and say hello. The secret is to make sure you're the first one in the office the day you've chosen for the meeting. This needs to be a speedy encounter.
- **Behavior:** Project warmth and good humor by smiling, making and maintaining eye contact, and offering a firm handshake. While this is supposed to be a casual conversation, don't forget to remain respectful and humble. If you can find a spot to offer some subtle flattery, feel free.

1. Meeting with a New Boss

Icebreaker: Mr. Green? Hi. We haven't been formally introduced yet, but I didn't want to wait any longer to welcome you. I'm Sean Curtis, manager of the publicity department.

Wants to talk now: *I've been meaning to look you up, Sean. Come in, please, and sit down. Let's go over some of the issues I understand your department has been wrestling with.*

Stall for time: I'm sorry. I have a client conference in a few minutes. Can you fill me in briefly on your priorities now? Then I'll be sure to bring the right information, along with some related ideas I've been developing, when we do talk.

Mentions a problem: *Frankly, I'm concerned with the size of our payroll, and I'd like to take a really hard look at your staffing.*

Probes for more: *Thanks for stopping by, Sean. I hear your department is one of the busiest in the company. Is this purely a social visit, or is there something specific you want to discuss?*

Elicit ideas: I don't want to tie you up with a long conversation now, but I was hoping to get a quick sense of your priorities for the department. I'll work specifically on those and be prepared when you have more time to talk.

Remains noncommittal: *I'd prefer to hear from you first. After all, you're a lot more familiar with the agenda in your department than I am.*

Gives the brushoff: *It's nice to meet you, Sean. I'd like to talk with you, but right now I'm very busy settling in. Why don't you stop by my office again later in the week.*

Float suggestion: Of course. For now, let me just quickly mention that I've been looking into ways to promote our image more aggressively and really get our name into the marketplace. I'll go into more detail once you've had a chance to catch your breath.

Appreciates input: *That could be an interesting discussion. Why don't you run some numbers and outline the specifics to me in a memo.*

Agree and set up meeting: I'd be happy to. I'll check with your assistant to set up a convenient time when we can talk in more detail. I think we can improve results. But for now, I just want to say welcome—we're happy to have you on board.

ADAPTATIONS

This script can be modified to:
- Introduce yourself to a newly elected official.
- Welcome a new neighbor.
- Introduce yourself to your child's new teacher.
- Conduct a reconnaissance before a major business meeting.

KEY POINTS

- Start by simply introducing yourself and offering a welcome.
- If you're brushed off or having trouble getting a hint, float a suggestion in order to get a response.
- If the new boss probes to see if there's more to your sudden appearance, honestly say you'd like to get a sense of his priorities.
- If he wants to talk right then, beg off, blaming it on a client or customer. You don't want to take the chance of making a mistake because of your lack of knowledge and preparation.
- If he mentions a problem, don't get defensive. Instead, handle it the same as if he simply offered a topic for future discussion.

Asking Your Boss for a Raise 2.

STRATEGY

While it has never been tougher to get a raise than today, it's still possible. The key is to realize there are only three acceptable reasons anymore: Your contributions to the company's bottom line have increased dramatically; your responsibilities have outgrown your job description; or your income hasn't kept pace with the going rate for individuals with your skills and experience. Using and documenting one of these arguments, and forcing your supervisor to fall back on a poverty excuse, will at least result in your obtaining further nonfinancial compensation or a deferred promise. And sometimes, that's the best you can hope for.

TACTICS

- **Attitude:** Remember that your salary has nothing to do with your value as a human being. It is solely a reflection of what your supervisor or company is willing to pay for your services. It's an entirely economic issue.
- **Preparation:** It's essential to have irrefutable documentation that backs up whichever of the three arguments you're using. When it comes to documenting industrywide salary ranges, draw on trade magazine surveys, headhunters, and professional associations. All your information should be included in a memo, with appropriate attachments, that outlines your argument.
- **Timing:** The best times to ask are shortly after a positive evaluation, upon successful completion of an important project, or after receiving some third-party recognition, such as an award. Avoid Mondays and Fridays entirely. Ask for an appointment either before business hours or just after lunch. The former will offer fewer interruptions; the latter will find your boss more relaxed.
- **Behavior:** It's completely up to you to blow your own horn, so avoid humility and subservience. Don't project guilt—you're asking for what you deserve. This forthright attitude will come through if you maintain direct eye contact whenever listening or speaking. Only break eye contact when you're thinking. Avoid nodding reflexively. Your agreement is powerful, especially in this situation. Let your boss fill in gaps in the conversation. Chattiness will imply insecurity. Speak only when necessary, and you'll convey strength and confidence.

2. Asking Your Boss for a Raise

Icebreaker: I'd like to thank you for the opportunity you and the company have given me. I recognize that you've been very influential in my growth and advancement. However, I have a problem that I need your help with.

Pitch #1: What has happened is that I've been concentrating solely on my professional growth and haven't been paying any attention to my stream of income. So I've done some research and found my peers in the industry are earning on average 15 percent more than my current compensation. I've drafted this memo that shows what I've found. It's logical for my compensation to keep pace with my growth. To do that I'll need an increase of [state increase].

Pitch #2: I think my salary no longer reflects my contribution to the company. In the past year, I've helped the company save a great deal of money [or] bring in added revenue [or] trim quite a bit from the cost of operations. I've done some research and I've found that a salary of [state salary] would more accurately reflect my value. I've prepared a brief memo outlining my accomplishments and my request.

Pitch #3: I think my salary no longer matches my job responsibilities. During the past year, I've moved from being an order taker to helping supervise the evening sales staff and helping draft the new selling scripts. I've done some research and I think a salary of [state salary] would more accurately reflect my responsibilities. I've prepared a brief memo outlining my increased responsibilities and my request.

Facts are wrong: *I can't believe you're underpaid. Let me take a look at your numbers. These figures come from companies larger than ours. If you check with companies the same size as ours you'll find you're making exactly what you should.*

Not enough time: *I won't argue your point. You've done an excellent job. But you simply haven't been here long enough [or] it simply hasn't been long enough since your last increase for you to merit a raise.*

Don't have the money: *I agree you've been doing a wonderful job. But as you know, business has been slow. The company simply doesn't have the money for raises right now [or] doesn't have that kind of money right now.*

Wouldn't be fair: *I agree with you completely. We've been very happy with your work. But we have a policy of.... How can I pay you more than Jean Smith, for instance, when she has worked here two years longer than you have?*

Solicit other sources: I don't want what I'm not entitled to. If my research is incomplete I'll be happy to do some more and come back to you with it, let's say, in two weeks. What companies would you consider comparable to ours?

Time is unfair measure: I really don't think you can fairly measure my contribution to the company by the amount of time I've been here [or] by how long it has been since my last raise. Let me go over the contributions I've outlined in my memo.

Expand the discussion: I understand. You can't do the impossible. But perhaps we can agree to an increase that would take effect, let's say, in six months. Meanwhile, there are some non-financial areas I need to speak with you about. For instance, I'd like another five vacation days....

Seniority is unfair measure: I've always assumed that excellent performance and taking on added responsibility would be rewarded in this company. I don't think it's fair to deny rewarding me for my contributions because of my lack of seniority. Let me go over the contributions I've outlined in my memo.

Won't offer sources: *I'd have to think about it. I'm really not sure. But I am sure you're not underpaid.*

Offers other sources: *Why don't you try looking at Smith & Jones and Pinnacle. They're both about our size. When you get numbers from them we'll talk again.*

Agrees to expand: *I can't guarantee the money will be there in another six months either. We'll have to see. But the added vacation days shouldn't be a problem.*

Refuses to expand: *I don't think either will be possible. The money may not be there in another six months, and adding to your vacation would be contrary to company policy. You'll have to wait.*

Seize initiative: I'll look into it further, and take the type of companies you suggested into account. Then, I'll come back to you with more results. Meanwhile, let's nail down that meeting. How about two weeks from today?

Ask for another meeting: I understand. But I need to leave here with a definite date for our next discussion. How about four months from today? Also, I'd appreciate your double-checking about those vacation days. [Start looking for another job.]

ADAPTATIONS

This script can be modified to:
- Obtain consideration for a promotion to another department or get a title changed.
- Get your employer to pay for continuing education.

KEY POINTS

- Begin by stressing that you love your job or company, but you have a problem you need help with.
- Your argument is that your compensation doesn't match your growth, contribution, or responsibilities.
- If your numbers are called into question, ask where you can get "correct" numbers. If none are offered, suggest some of your own and ask for a follow-up meeting.
- If your boss says insufficient time has passed from some other event, say time isn't relevant to your growth, contribution, or responsibilities.
- If fairness to others is cited, say that compensation based solely on seniority is also unfair.
- If your boss pleads poverty, ask for nonfinancial compensation and/or a future agreement.
- If you're stonewalled, force a future meeting and start looking for another job.

Asking Your Boss for a Promotion

STRATEGY

Asking for a promotion is even more difficult than asking for a raise. That's because you have to demonstrate not only that you have the skills to handle the new position, but also that leaving your current job won't hurt either your boss or the company. The secret is to prepare two plans of action: one for the new position and one for your current job. Don't fall back on seniority or hierarchy to make your case—they don't hold water in today's business world. Focus on your proven ability to do the job and emphasize that you're ready to move up. One other essential: Make sure to present your case as soon as possible, preferably before an outside search has begun.

TACTICS

- **Attitude:** Look on this not as something you're owed for past services, but as an opportunity you've shown you're ready for. There are no entitlements in today's workplace.
- **Preparation:** Draft two formal memos—one outlining what you'd do in the first ninety days in the new job and another explaining how you'd assist whoever takes over your current position. In addition, have in mind potential replacements for your position.
- **Timing:** It is absolutely essential to stake your claim to the job as soon as you hear it's available. Consider dropping hints and spreading the word informally, if you can do it without looking pushy. The more time that passes, the less your chances of landing the job.
- **Behavior:** Accept compliments and constructive criticism gracefully, but don't hesitate to argue around these points by directing the conversation to your strengths rather than to your weaknesses.

3. Asking Your Boss for a Promotion

Icebreaker and pitch: I understand Keith is leaving. I'm hoping that you'll seriously consider me for his job. Since he and I have worked so closely together over the past year, I'm very familiar with the department and what's required. And when I've filled in for Keith, I think I've shown that I can manage the staff effectively.

Going outside: *I appreciate your interest in the position, but we've decided that we need a completely fresh approach. That's why we're looking outside the company for a replacement.*

Need you where you are: *You've been doing an outstanding job in your position—that's exactly why I can't afford to move you right now. I need you where you are.*

You're not ready: *You've shown tremendous growth over the past year, but you don't have enough experience yet with customer service or with managing a staff to take on a job like Keith's.*

Have fresh approach: I think I can offer a fresh approach—and at a much lower cost than if you go outside the company. I have a lot of ideas that I think could really reenergize the staff. And after four years in my current job, I'm eager for a new challenge.

Will help train: Thank you. I appreciate your confidence in me. But I'd be happy to work closely with my replacement until he's completely familiar with my system. In fact, I can suggest people in my department who would be great for the job.

Have inside knowledge: I may not have been at it along time, but I think I've shown a real flair for customer service. Even more importantly, I know how this department works, inside and out. You won't get that kind of experience if you go outside.

No more money: *You understand that if I do put you in the position, I probably won't be able to give you a salary increase.*

Let me think about it: *I can't make you any promises, but I'll think about what you said and get back to you.*

Offer memo: Thank you. Making this move is just as important to me as joining the company was. I'll put my ideas for the department in a memo and have it on your desk tomorrow.

I'm flexible: I'm most interested in my prospects over the long term. I'd be willing to take a little bit less right now than the job normally pays if we can accelerate the timetable for my next raise—provided you're satisfied with my work.

ADAPTATIONS

This script can be modified to:
- Request a transfer.
- Move ahead in a political or social organization.
- Broadcast your ambitions and willingness for more responsibility.

KEY POINTS

- Acknowledge you've heard there's an opening, state your qualifications, and ask directly to be considered for the job.
- Respond to arguments for going outside by demonstrating how you can bring a fresh approach—at a lower cost.
- Don't let your success be used against you. Offer to work with your replacement.
- Claims that you don't have sufficient seniority can be met by showing how your time, while short, has been intensive, and by showing exactly what is necessary to do the job.
- Be prepared to forgo a raise—at least until you've proven yourself.
- Have a memo ready outlining your plans.

Asking Your Boss for a Transfer

STRATEGY

The most important aspect of this dialogue is knowing that your boss's primary concern is how your transfer will affect her. Although you're excited about the prospect of a new city and working with different people, your boss is calculating the impact of your departure. Keep your boss's point of view in mind, and you'll be able to successfully navigate this conversation. First, be sure you're transferring to a location where they need someone with your skills. You can't transfer somewhere where you're not needed. Be certain to give your boss sufficient time to consider your transfer request. The more advance notice you give, the more likely she is to approve your request. Soothe your boss's worst fear by assuring her you'll work with your replacement. Emphasize you don't want to leave your department understaffed. If your timetable is flexible, offer to stay until your replacement is working at maximum efficiency. Your boss will appreciate your loyalty and take the offer as a gesture of good faith. Your boss may insist a transfer is impossible until several key projects are completed. Be ready to compromise—but don't get bullied into an unreasonable agreement. Stress you're transferring for a career opportunity, improved lifestyle, or other pertinent reason, and not because of dissatisfaction with your job. If pressed, suggest promoting a younger employee to take your place. Promoting from within will save the company time and money, not to mention to clear the way for your transfer. Manage your boss's fear and anticipate her objections, and you'll get your transfer.

TACTICS

- **Attitude:** Be flexible, but within reason. You're asking for something that could weaken your department, so be ready to compromise. Thank your boss for the opportunity of working with her. It may seem transparent flattery, but it will set a friendly tone for the dialogue.
- **Timing:** Request the transfer as soon as a position becomes available at the new office. Your boss needs time to replace you and time for you to work with your replacement.
- **Preparation:** Check the company's policies regarding transfers. Research any transfers that took place during the past year. Find out if the company will pay your moving costs.
- **Behavior:** Emphasize that transferring is critical and your decision final. If you approach your boss with a half-baked idea, she'll deny your transfer. Whatever the reason, make it seem that there's nothing more important than your transferring.

15

4. Asking Your Boss for a Transfer

Icebreaker: First, I'd like to tell you how much I enjoy working in this department. I've learned a lot and will always be grateful to you. There's a position at main headquarters that would present me with a fantastic career opportunity [or] wonderful lifestyle change. As much as I hate to leave this office, I'd like to request a transfer.

Angry: *Headquarters doesn't need you, we do. Just when we get busy you turn your back on us. I'm not approving any transfer request.*

Panic: *You know the summer report is coming up and we can't be shorthanded. You have too many responsibilities here. I can't transfer you right now.*

Apathetic: *You have to do what you think is best for your career. You can coordinate things with headquarters, but don't expect any help from me.*

Helpful: *That's great. Of course, I'm sorry to lose a valued employee, but I understand you have to think about your career. Why don't we discuss how your career. Why don't we discuss how we can best smooth the transition.*

Soothe anger: I understand your concern, but I don't intend to abandon your department. I'd like to be responsible for training my replacement. I don't plan on moving until I can be sure my replacement will work out.

Calm panic: I haven't forgotten about the summer report. That's why I intend to work hard training my replacement. The last thing I want to do is leave you understaffed, but this opportunity may not come along again. I won't leave until we both agree my replacement is working out.

Sorry: I'm sorry I won't be able to count on your assistance. I have great respect for you and appreciate everything I've learned. I hope you'll allow me to work closely with my replacement to make the transition easier.

Share ideas: Working closely with my replacement, I can insure a smooth transition period. I'd also like to write a departure memo detailing the tasks to be completed for the summer report. If you have any other ideas, I'd love to hear them.

Delay: I understand what you're saying, but I don't think I can approve a transfer until the summer report is done. I'm sorry, this is the busy time of year and I can't weaken my department.

Not sure: Even if you work with a replacement it will take a long time before that person is fully contributing. First we have to find someone qualified and then spend time training them. The entire process takes longer than you think. This just isn't a good time for you to transfer.

Fair: OK. What kind of time table are you thinking about? If you're willing to work with me, then I'm willing to help you. But it has to be reasonable.

Good guy: I appreciate your offering to work with your replacement. I'd also like to keep you available by telephone after the transfer. That way, if any questions come up we can give you a call.

Alternative: I have an idea that could save time and money. I've been working with Sweeney. She's a quick learner and a sharp young woman. I think she's ready to step into my position. If you promote from within, the department will save time and money.

Compromise: If I don't transfer now I may miss my chance. I'll work with my replacement, extend my hours, and work on weekends. I'm willing to give an extra effort if it means helping the department and getting the transfer approved.

Your plan: I want to spend two or three weeks training my replacement. Following a short evaluation period, you and I can discuss her performance. If everything goes well, I can transfer shortly thereafter.

Success: That sounds great. I appreciate your input and support. As soon as you have a replacement lined up, I'd like to begin training them. Thanks again for your help.

Interesting: That's not a bad idea. Sweeney may be ready. You'll be responsible for working with her and getting her ready for the summer report. If she doesn't work out, you'll have to delay your transfer.

No: I'm sorry, but I don't agree with your logic or suggestions. This is an important time and we can't afford to be without you. I sympathize with your situation, but you'll have to wait at least a couple of months before I can consider a transfer.

Absorb rejection: I understand your position. [See Lifescript 19: Going over your boss's head.]

Yes: OK. If you follow through on your promises I don't see any reason to stand in your way. I expect you to make this a smooth transition. I'll approve your transfer provided your replacement is contributing.

Thanks: I know this can work out for both of us. Thanks for meeting with me. I appreciate your support.

ADAPTATIONS

This script can be modified to:

- Ask for a recommendation for another job.

KEY POINTS

- Be sure you're requesting a transfer to a place you're needed.
- Emphasize how important the transfer is to you and your family.
- Stress that you like your job, but need to transfer because of your family, your career, a lifestyle change, or some other important reason.
- Offer to work extra hours and on weekends, if that means being transferred within a reasonable amount of time.
- Suggest a younger employee for promotion. This will satisfy your boss and speed your transfer.
- If you don't get support, express your thanks and go over your boss's head.

Asking Your Boss for Flextime

5.

STRATEGY

One excellent solution to the child-care dilemma is for one or both parents to arrange flexible hours, or "flextime," with their employers. While these are tough sells, especially to conservative employers, they can be accomplished. The secrets are to approach this as a rehire since, in effect, you're redefining your job status; to stress your commitment to the company, especially in light of your being a parent; and to "yes" your employer to death, showing your willingness to assume every cost or burden yourself. Of course, the more valuable you are to the company, the more likely you are to get the schedule you want.

TACTICS

- **Attitude:** Realize that you're asking your employer to break company tradition as well as give up some control over you. That means it's essential to let him retain the feeling that he's still in charge.
- **Preparation:** First, ascertain your value to the company. Second, develop a plan that will let you accomplish as much, if not more, than before. Third, determine exactly which office or communications equipment you'll need to be able to do your job, and be ready to assume the cost. Fourth, think of every possible objection to your plan and have a solution ready—even if it means taking a temporary salary reduction. And fifth, draft a cogent, eloquent memo outlining your proposal.
- **Timing:** If you're already on parental leave, this meeting should take place before you actually return to work. If you haven't yet left on leave, postpone the meeting until you're ready to return. If you're not going on leave, have the meeting as soon as possible.
- **Behavior:** Express your gratitude to your supervisor and the company, but don't come off as a supplicant. Act as if you are on a job interview—confident and eager. Treat this as a business arrangement, not a favor. Sure, you're asking for something, but you're ready to make concessions in order to get it. If possible, let your supervisor have the last word—that will reaffirm his feeling of being in charge.

5. Asking Your Boss for Flextime

Icebreaker: I wanted to tell you how much I've looked forward to coming back to work. Being away these past two months has reinforced how strongly I feel about my job here. That's why I wanted to meet with you today.

Pitch: I think I've figured out a way to balance my obligations to my family and my responsibilities on the job. By working at home on Mondays and Fridays, I'll be able to resolve my child-care problems and fulfill all my work duties. On Tuesdays, Wednesdays, and Thursdays, I'll be able to attend staff meetings, sit in on planning sessions, and meet with clients and editors. Mondays and Fridays I'll concentrate on preparing press kits and releases and making follow-up calls to editors. I'll be able to accomplish as much as I did before, if not more, and I can guarantee the quality of my work won't suffer.

Feasibility objection: *I know you feel strongly about your job—but you wouldn't be human if you didn't put your child first. I can't see how you're going to be able to concentrate on your work while you're at home with your son.*

Precedent objection: *I don't doubt what you're saying. But if I make this kind of arrangement with you I'd have to do it with everyone else in the company who'd rather work at home. I'm sorry but I can't afford to set a precedent.*

Salary objection: *You may be able to do your job that way, but how am I going to justify your putting in less time here, while still making the same money? I know it's results that count, but the people upstairs and your coworkers watch the clock.*

Cost objection: *I just don't see how you're going to be able to do your job from home without a tremendous amount of equipment. I don't think the company would be willing to foot the bill for what you'd need.*

Explain your backup: I thought of that, too. I spoke with my husband, and he has agreed to care for our son in the morning and evening. My mother-in-law has also offered to help. While I may not be able to work uninterrupted during the afternoons, with their help I'll be able to devote mornings and evenings to my work.

Make it an exception: This would let me continue to deliver the kind of performance you've praised me for in the past. Rather than a precedent, I think it's simply an exception. And I've always been under the impression the company makes exceptions to policy when it's to its benefit.

Make a concession: I also think it's productivity, not hours, that counts. But I know the kinds of pressures you're under. That's why I'd be willing to accept slightly less in salary, with the understanding that if my work is outstanding, as it has been in the past, I'll receive a year-end bonus that compensates for the salary reduction.

Assume the necessary cost: You're right. The equipment isn't cheap. But my husband and I decided it was a worthwhile investment and have already bought it ourselves. We picked up a computer and fax/modem and have set up a home office. All we need to do is add another telephone line and buy the appropriate software.

Won't budge: *I'm sorry. I'm just not convinced you'll be able to deliver on what you're saying [or] I don't think I'm going to be able to get the people upstairs to go along with us on this idea.*

Same standards: *Okay, we'll give it a shot. But I just want you to know that I'm going to hold you and your work to the same high standards as I did before. I don't want to see the slightest decrease in your performance.*

Trial run: *All right. I'll be willing to have a trial run for, let's say, six months. But I want you to understand that I'm making no guarantee about the future. If you can't deliver we'll have to reexamine the situation.*

It's your money: *I'm sure there will be other hurdles, but as long as you understand the company won't be responsible for your costs and you can guarantee the same level of productivity I'm willing to give it a try.*

Experiment: All I'd like is the opportunity to prove myself. Let's try this as an experiment for, say, three months. If at the end of that time you're still not convinced, I'll give up the idea and go along with your decision. Does that sound agreeable?

Volunteer as advocate: I know how tough they can be. With your permission, I'll draft a memo outlining my proposal and pitch it to them myself. If you could help me with that memo and at the meeting, I'd really appreciate it. Why don't we give them a call.

Thank you: That sounds fair. Thanks for all your help. I promise you won't be disappointed.

ADAPTATIONS

This script can be modified to:
- Obtain independent contractor status.
- Obtain part-time status.

KEY POINTS

- Stress that you love your job more than ever now that you've been away from it—that's why you're asking for the meeting.
- Your argument should be that you've figured out a way to balance your "obligations" to the job with your "responsibilities" to your child.
- If your supervisor reflexively says your plan isn't feasible, describe how your plan addresses every contingency.
- If your supervisor says he can't set a precedent, frame the arrangement as an exception, not a new rule.
- If your supervisor says he can't justify paying you the same as before, agree to a temporary salary concession, but ask for a year-end bonus if you maintain your productivity.
- If your supervisor objects to the cost, offer to assume it yourself.
- If your supervisor still refuses, ask for a short trial period.
- If your supervisor expresses fear of higher-ups, volunteer to present the proposal yourself.

Asking Your Boss for Maternity Leave

STRATEGY

This dialogue isn't about what your boss is saying, but what she's not saying. While she will congratulate you, what she really wants to know is how long you'll be gone and how your departure will affect the company. Your boss may be worried you'll never return from leave. Your goal is protecting your job while you're gone. Though in most cases your position will be protected—that's the law—lots of things can happen while you are on leave, particularly if you're in a competitive industry or company. You've worked hard and taking maternity leave should not diminish your status in the company. Address your boss's fears and concerns and you'll be able to protect your standing in the company.

TACTICS

- **Attitude:** Display concern. Your boss will be worried about the effect of your absence. If you share her concern, it will make the situation easier to negotiate.
- **Timing:** Set an appointment early in the week to speak with your boss in private. Make sure she hears about your pregnancy from you and not through the grapevine. Naturally, you cannot set an exact date for your leave, but the more advance notice the better.
- **Preparation:** Speak subtly with coworkers who have taken leave and check the company policies prior to your meeting. Review your current workload and create a strategy for sharing your responsibilities with other employees.
- **Behavior:** Although you're conveying good news, your boss may view it as bad. Don't smile and celebrate during the meeting; you should be serious and concerned about the company. Your boss will appreciate your unselfish approach to the situation.

6. Asking Your Boss for Maternity Leave

Icebreaker: Thanks for meeting with me. My job is very important to me and for that reason I wanted you to be the first in the office to know I'm pregnant. I'd like to talk to you about taking maternity leave.

Friendly: *That's great news. When are you due?*

Practical: *Congratulations. When are you planning to take leave? We'll need to talk about what to do with your work.*

All-business: *Oh, I see. We'll miss you. Perhaps you and I should discuss hiring your replacement [or] dividing up your work?*

Skeptical: *Oh, how nice for you. Now, is this really a request for temporary leave? A lot of mothers say they're going to come back, but never really do. If that's the case, I'd like to know now.*

Stay focused: Thank you, it's not for another five months. What I'd really like to discuss is how I can best help the company remain productive while I'm on leave.

Unveil plan: I'm glad you mentioned that because I would like to help the company prepare for my leave.

No replacement: You certainly won't need to hire a replacement. The company should be able to compensate for my temporary absence by hiring a temp [or] dividing up my work.

Leave is temporary: Oh, I'm coming back. I'd like to discuss how I can help contribute to the company while on leave.

Open-minded: *Well, the company policy is to provide six weeks of maternity leave…but if you need more time I'm happy to listen to it.*

Pandering: *Let us worry about finding someone to do your work. You should be thinking about your baby. Your work will still be here when you get back.*

Inflexible: *The company offers six weeks of leave. We've always brought in outside help and divided up the individual's work among others.*

Get follow-up: If it's all right with you, I'd like to schedule a meeting for a couple of weeks prior to my due date to discuss the specifics of my leave.

ADAPTATIONS

The script can be modified to:
- Request leave to care for an elderly parent.
- Request leave to care for a sick child.

KEY POINTS

- Dismiss any notion that you won't return or need to be replaced.
- Show concern for the effect your leave will have on the company.
- Emphasize the importance of your job and your commitment to your career.

Asking Your Boss for Paternity Leave

7.

STRATEGY

The problem with requesting paternity leave is that history isn't on your side. While you've just as much legal right to parental leave as a mother, society in general, and employers in particular, don't view things that way. Women are expected to place their family first. Men are not. Your goal here is to get sufficient leave without weakening your position in the company. Customarily, companies offer shorter paternity leave than maternity leave, and that can actually work in your favor. Still, your boss may accuse you of leaving at a crucial time, since there's never a good time to take leave. To mitigate objections, suggest working part-time at home and calling the office daily. Stress you don't see this as a vacation, and show your boss you want to continue to contribute to the company. Offer to work with other coworkers who will share your assignments during the leave, but be certain such arrangements are temporary. Volunteer to come to the office one day over the weekend and do some work. Whatever you can do to meet your boss halfway will ultimately be appreciated and smooth the effects of your paternity leave.

TACTICS

- **Attitude:** Be flexible, but not a pushover. You're entitled to this leave; just negotiate a mutually beneficial agreement and your boss will be satisfied.
- **Timing:** Request leave well before your wife's due date. The more advance warning, the less your boss can protest. Try to approach him after you have successfully completed a project or done something beneficial for the company.
- **Preparation:** Check around the office to see if any other fathers have taken leave. Find out how they were treated and check your employee handbook regarding terms of the leave. Have specific ideas about staying in touch with work.
- **Behavior:** Be ready to compromise on terms, but not on timing. You must be granted the leave, it's just a question of the effects it has on your career. Be firm, but open-minded.

7. Asking Your Boss for Paternity Leave

Icebreaker: As you may know, my wife is pregnant. She's due in about two months, and I'd like to speak to you about my paternity leave. My wife is going to take her leave first, so I'll be beginning my leave in four months.

Angry: *That's right around the Fall Show! That would be a terrible time to take off. We can't afford to lose any time on our fall projects.*

Threatening: *I can't stop you from taking leave, but I'll have to reassign your work.*

Delay: *Can't you postpone your leave until the winter? Maybe your wife can get an extension. You know how important the fall season is to us.*

Worried: *Naturally, you can take leave. I'm just concerned about the impact your absence will have on the company.*

Team player: Oh, I don't plan on leaving work completely. I want to arrange a part-time schedule with you. If I work from my home and come in on weekends, I don't think the office will suffer.

Keep your work: I don't think reassigning my work will be necessary. I can still contribute by working part-time from my home and coming in on weekends. I'm committed to my job and won't be losing touch with the office.

Can't delay: My wife will already have expended her leave, so I'm afraid I can't postpone mine, but I would like to work part-time from home and come in on weekends. That way I can continue to contribute on a daily basis.

Share concern: I'm concerned myself. That's why I'd like to work part-time from my home and come in on the weekend. I'm sure that will ease the impact of my absence.

Bad example: *If I don't at least hire a temporary replacement for you or divide up your responsibilities I'll be setting a new precedent. I'm afraid I just can't do that.*

Unrealistic: *Believe me, parenthood isn't as easy as you think. I've been there. If you're taking leave to care for a newborn, you're not going to find time to work.*

Just leave: *I think you should just take the regular three weeks-full-time leave. A part-time or home-based employee will just be a distraction to everyone else.*

Positive example: I understand your position, but if we set up an effective strategy for continuing to work while on leave, it can only be a positive precedent, not a negative one.

Well planned: I really have thought this plan through. My in-laws have volunteered to watch the baby while I dedicate a few hours a day to work. With their help, I can be productive working at home.

Address his fear: I agree it would be a slight adjustment, but I think it's worth a try. Even part-time I can still be productive for the company.

Agrees: *OK, you convinced me. I appreciate your dedication. I'm willing to give your plan a try.*

Rejects offer: *You can take your leave, but we'll be dividing up your work [or] hiring a temp to help fill in for you.*

Maybe: *Let me think about your idea and get back to you.*

Follow-up: Let's schedule another meeting in a month. We can iron out the specifics then.

ADAPTATIONS

This script can be modified to:
- Request leave to care for an ill family member.
- Request time off after elective surgery.

KEY POINTS
- Emphasize the importance of your career.
- Do not accept any delays. Tell your boss when you're taking the leave, not the other way around.
- Point out the positive effects of your plan. Convince your boss he would be setting a fine example by granting you part-time leave at home.
- No matter what the outcome, schedule a meeting to discuss your leave again in a month. If your boss disagrees with your plan, use this follow-up meeting to try again.

Asking Your Boss for Emergency Leave

8.

STRATEGY

Unless yours is a company with an established procedure for emergency leaves, you'll need to ask your supervisor directly for time off. Be forewarned that some supervisors, despite their protestations, will be much more concerned with the effect your absence will have on the bottom line than with your personal problem. The secret to this dialogue is to make it clear you have no choice but to take the time off, but that your workload can be adequately handled either by others or through your remaining in constant touch with the office. Feel free to be a bit abrupt—it's apt to trigger a reflexive probe into what's wrong that immediately establishes a sympathetic tone to the dialogue. While you may be able to fend off attempts to turn your emergency leave into your vacation, when push comes to shove, you'll have to accept that unless your supervisor is both powerful and gracious. You also may have to forgo salary while you're away. Your goal here is to get the time off, and, if at all possible, to keep your vacation.

TACTICS

- **Attitude:** In your heart of hearts, you must feel this is a true emergency—otherwise you won't convey the necessary sense of urgency to carry the day. You must be able to say honestly you have no choice.
- **Preparation:** Before having this conversation, make sure that you have plans—including detailed memos—in place to handle any workplace problems that could arise, and that your current projects are all in good shape.
- **Timing:** To the extent possible, have this conversation as early in the day and as early in the workweek as you can. Try contacting your staff or whoever will be filling in for you before working hours so contingency plans are already in place when it comes time to meet the boss.
- **Behavior:** The more concerned and determined you are to take a leave of absence, and the more willing you are to do whatever needs to be done to get the time off, the smoother this dialogue will go.

8. Asking Your Boss for Emergency Leave

Icebreaker: I have a family problem, and I need an emergency leave of absence. I'll need to be away for three weeks.

Asks for details: *Slow down. First, tell me what's wrong. What happened?*

Explain situation: My aunt passed away unexpectedly, and her affairs are in a shambles. She has no children and there's no one else in the family with the ability to handle it. I've already spoken to my assistant, Pat, about all pending matters. All our projects are in good shape, and I'll be in touch daily by telephone, fax, and e-mail.

Gives grudging approval: *Well, as long as you're right and things are under control and you'll be in touch, I don't have a problem with it. Just try to be back as soon as possible.*

Use your vacation time: *Well, you do have two weeks of vacation coming to you, although I'd prefer having had notice about when you'd be taking it. As for the third week, we'll work it out; maybe we can take it from next year's vacation.*

Not a vacation: I'd really rather not lose my vacation time for a family emergency. After all, it's not like I won't be working, and I will be in constant touch with the office. I was hoping the company wouldn't penalize me for the death of my aunt.

Won't take authority: *I can't make a decision like that on my own. Whether or not you'll be working, you won't be here. And if you're not here and you're not on vacation I can't pay you...at least not without approval from upstairs.*

OK, but no pay: *OK, as long as you keep on top of things, I think we'll be able to give you an unpaid leave of absence. Just try to get back here as soon as possible.*

Offer to go upstairs: I'd appreciate it then if you'd go upstairs and tell them I really have no choice. If you'd prefer, I'll approach them directly. But I'd appreciate it if you back me up.

Accept conditions: I really have no choice in the matter. I'll be back as soon as I can.

ADAPTATIONS

This script can be modified to:
- Get an extended leave of absence to wind up family business.
- Get a medical leave for elective surgery.

KEY POINTS

- Present your request for time off prior to divulging the details of the emergency. This forces your boss to ask what's wrong, potentially setting up a humane tone for the meeting.
- Stress that all your work is under control and that you'll be available should any problems arise.
- Fend off any attempts to take away vacation time by suggesting that it would constitute unfair punishment for something that's beyond your control.
- If your boss claims she's powerless, offer to take your case to higher-ups, but ask for her support.
- If you're forced to go without pay, demonstrate the urgency of the matter by accepting the condition.

Asking Your Boss for a Deadline Extension

9

STRATEGY

The secret to asking for a deadline extension is to make it clear that your only problem is time; nothing else is wrong. Rather than coming in to your supervisor with an apology and series of reasons why you're not going to be able to meet the established deadline, steer the discussion as quickly as possible to solutions. The schedule established was clearly unworkable, and now you need help in coming up with ways to deal with the situation. Offer alternatives, but make it clear that delivery as intended is impossible.

TACTICS

- **Attitude:** This is a time neither to fall on your own sword nor to assign blame to others. It's not important who or what is to blame. What's important is deciding the next step. The more you adopt this attitude, the more likely your supervisor will as well.
- **Preparation:** Don't waste time determining why you won't be able to deliver on time—invariably, it's because the schedule was overly optimistic. There's nothing you can do about it now. Instead, come up with as many alternative solutions as you can. There are usually three variations: getting more time, hiring outside help to deliver on time, or submitting a draft on the due date with the final product to follow later. Be prepared to advocate one alternative over the others in case your supervisor is unwilling to take responsibility.
- **Timing:** It's essential you have this conversation as soon as you realize you're not going to meet your deadline. Procrastination can only hurt you because you don't know if there are other issues involved. The sooner you realize the deadline is unworkable and convey that to your supervisor, the better. The longer you wait, the more this will look like a failing on your part.
- **Behavior:** Remain objective and rational. Don't let anger put you on the defensive or fear get the better of you. You, your supervisor, the project, and the company will all best be served by your continuing to steer the conversation around to solutions rather than postmortems.

9. Asking Your Boss for a Deadline Extension

Icebreaker: We need to talk about the Jackson project. It can't be completed in the thirty days we have available. I need your help in coming up with a solution.

Calm but curious: *What went wrong?*

Nervous: *Time is of the essence. I've committed us to that delivery date.*

Angry: *I should have known better than to rely on you for something this important.*

Disappointed: *I relied on your promises. This is a real letdown.*

Was simply unworkable: In retrospect, it's clear our original timetable simply wasn't workable. But I think I have some workable solutions.

Don't panic: I don't think we need to panic. I think I have some workable solutions.

Absorb anger: Your anger is understandable, but let's focus on solving the problem. I think I have some workable solutions.

Absorb disappointment: I understand and share your disappointment. But I think I have some workable solutions.

Present plans: I think we have three options. The first, but costliest, option is to bring in an outside team of temps to work over the next four weekends. Obviously, I'd be willing to come in and supervise them. The second option is to get a fifteen-day extension from the client. The third option is to submit an outline and first draft of the project to the clients as soon as possible, solicit their comments and suggestions, saying their happiness is very important to us, and ask for additional time to incorporate those ideas into the finished project.

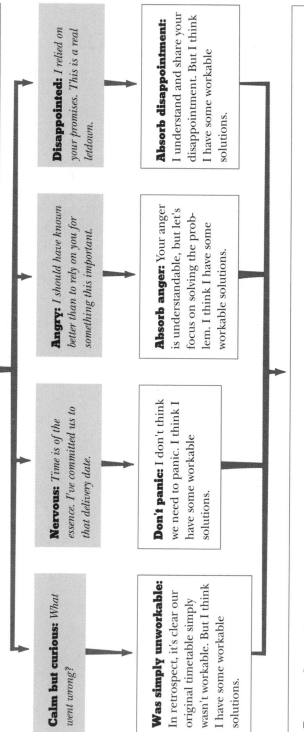

Still hesitant: *That's all very well, but you've left us in an awkward position with the client, not being able to deliver on time.*

Gives a cushion: *Okay. I'll take care of the client. You take another fifteen days. Just make sure you deliver a first-class product.*

Needs time to choose: *Good thinking. Those are three viable options. Let me give it some thought and get back to you on which way we'll go.*

Suggest your choice: I've been thinking about that, too. I've put together an outline and first draft. I think you'll agree it's an excellent start. I think that once we incorporate your changes, we may be able to show this to them and mitigate the damage.

Express admiration: The way you've handled this situation just reaffirms my admiration for your management skills. Thanks for your help.

ADAPTATIONS

This script can be modified to:
- Mollify a client or customer.
- Ask a client or customer for more time.

KEY POINTS

- Present the failure to meet the deadline as a given and go directly to offering alternative solutions.
- If you're asked for a reason, just say the schedule was unworkable and launch into your suggestions.
- If your supervisor expresses anxiety, anger, or disappointment, say these feelings are understandable, but immediately shift the topic to solutions.
- Solutions generally involve either getting more time, bringing in outside help, or presenting an outline on time with the finished product to follow later.
- If your supervisor seems unwilling to select from your set of solutions, be prepared to advocate one approach.

Asking Your Boss for Help with Your Workload

10.

STRATEGY

This delicate dialogue must be handled with care. Ask your boss for assistance and she may think you're an underachiever or a lazy employee. Even if you've taken on or accepted too much work, your boss may not recognize this. That's why you should only use this dialogue as a last resort, after all else has failed. That being said, the secret to this conversation is guiding the dialogue toward a solution. Don't let your boss turn the meeting into a review of your employment history. Remind her that you're doing good work, but there's just too much for one person. The fact that you recognize the work overload and are attempting to solve the problem is a sign of strength. It's entirely possible your boss is not aware of the enormous workload and may sympathize with your predicament. However, you should be ready to deflect anger or disappointment. This meeting should appear to be about your concern for the company and quality of your work. If you're unable to keep pace with an unreasonable workload, the company will ultimately suffer. Don't be passive and throw yourself on the mercy of your boss. Explore options and have possible alternatives prepared to discuss with your boss during the meeting. Show her you're eager to solve the problem early so the company isn't adversely affected.

TACTICS

- **Attitude:** Be concerned, but not intimidated. Be decisive. Act positively, deflect anger, and discuss solutions. You're seeking a solution, not an excuse.
- **Timing:** Speak with your boss the moment you realize there's too much work to handle. Procrastinating will make the situation worse. The moment your boss has any free time, you must pull her aside and alert her to your quandary.
- **Preparation:** Prepare a memo outlining your solution, and present the plan to your boss during the meeting so she can comment immediately.
- **Behavior:** Be direct and swift. Don't just throw up your hands and cry for help. Be active in the solution process. Remain calm, even if threatened, and present a positive solution that will benefit you and the company.

10. Asking Your Boss for Help with Your Workload

Icebreaker: I need your help in solving a potential problem. I've taken a close look at my workload and realize my enthusiasm has gotten the better of me. I've accepted too many assignments to keep up my usual high standards. I'm hoping we can discuss some possible solutions or alternatives.

Angry: *This is the last thing I need. I can't believe this. How far behind are you?*

Disappointed: *This is going to set us back. We don't have time for this. I was really counting on you.*

Threatening: *Perhaps someone else would be able to handle your workload. Maybe I should give Jones a try.*

Calm: *What do you think went wrong? You've always been a hard worker.*

Deflect anger: I'm not behind yet, but if things don't change, I will fall behind. Maybe you could help me identify the most important project I'm working on now so that I can complete my work on a priority basis.

Deflect disappointment: I agree that we can't waste time, but I don't think this is a setback. What I need is a little guidance. Perhaps you could set priorities for each project. That way my co-workers and I will be able to dedicate our time to the right assignment.

Respond to threat: I considered that, but I think Jones will run into the same problem I have—it's just too much work for one person to handle. If you could assign each project a priority rating, then I can work on each task in the order of importance.

Explain: I'm simply about to become overloaded. There's just more work here than there are hours in a day. If you evaluate each project on a priority basis, I could work through each assignment and not fall behind the deadlines.

Disagrees: *Look, you have to be multifaceted to work in this department. I can't hold your hand and point you in the right direction every day. You need to take some responsibility for your work.*

Agrees: *I think you're right. We need to get everyone on the same page. I didn't realize the confusion created by multiple deadlines. If the department understands the importance of each project do you think that will solve your overloading problem?*

Express thanks: Yes, absolutely. I knew coming to you would solve the problem. With your approval, I'll organize a meeting Monday morning to discuss the projects you think we should be concentrating on.

Disagrees somewhat: *It's just not that simple. Each project has subtle levels of importance. You have to work on multiple projects every day. Even if one project is on the front burner, others cannot be ignored.*

Agrees somewhat: *I see your point, but it would be difficult to set priorities for each project. It might be tough to realign the department on a priority basis.*

Convince boss: If everyone pitches in, it won't be too difficult. If you list the most important projects, then I can make sure I'm spending my hours on the correct project. The payoff is that assigning work on a priority basis will save time and money.

Sell the idea: I'm not suggesting we ignore any projects, but I think we can focus on the most important projects and no one person will be overwhelmed. If everyone cooperates, we can save time and money.

Stress your point: I understand your position, but if we can set priorities, then every one will be working at full capacity. I fear that I may not be the only employee who is overloaded. Eventually, the company is going to lose work, quality, and money.

Retreat and suggest compromise: If Jones and I could share the June report, then we can balance the workload. By combining our efforts, we can finish the report on time.

Final no: *I just think you need to apply yourself. If you can't handle the work, I'll give it to someone else. All our projects are of equal importance and we can't neglect any assignments. Now, what should we do about your situation?*

ADAPTATIONS

This script can be modified to:
- Ask a business partner to help you during a busy time.

KEY POINTS

- Remind your boss you're not an underachiever—there's just too much work for one person.
- Emphasize you're concerned about the quality of your work and the success of the company
- Don't tuck your tail between your legs and beg for help. Be proactive in the solution process.
- If your boss won't budge, suggest a specific alternative to lighten your workload.

Asking Your Boss for a Bigger or Better Workspace

11.

STRATEGY

With the increasing reliance of management on cubicle workspaces, getting a better workspace is entirely reliant on convincing your boss it will make you a more efficient worker. No superior is interested in vanity, ego, or a personal desire for a nice view, unless it affects his own vanity, ego, or desire. Consider that your boss cannot give you something that doesn't exist, so start by checking around the office to make sure there's a better space available. By having specific spaces in mind you can force your boss to comment on them, rather than your request in general. Your conversation must be about how a better space will maximize your work output. Explain that being crammed into a tiny space doesn't allow enough room for your files and documents, or for you to meet privately with clients or peers, or even to work efficiently. Tell your boss how much time is wasted in trying to maneuver and work in the small office, when the sensible answer would be to provide you with more space. Point out that you're not seeking a raise or promotion, just enough room to do your job. Deflect accusations that you're not utilizing your current space by assuring your boss you've tried every alternative, but are limited by the lack of room. After discussing the problems of a smaller space, explain how much more productive you'll be in a larger space. Describe how an improved space will allow you to work effectively, how much time will be saved in a practical and efficient space, and how you'll be able to meet with clients and coworkers. Your boss may suggest that giving you a better workspace will create jealousy among your peers. Steer him away from a dialogue about everyone else's feelings and back to a discussion about your specific situation. It's essential to illustrate how your workspace may soon negatively effect your job performance. Center the dialogue on the quality of your work, and your boss will understand the importance of moving you.

TACTICS

- **Attitude:** Be confident and concerned. Remind your boss this request is about your job performance, not your personal comfort. You're only concerned about the quality of your work.
- **Timing:** Approach the boss as soon as you discover a desirable space. Stake your claim immediately. Open offices are like vacuums; they demand to be filled. If you hesitate, one of your coworkers will be the one moving.

11. Asking Your Boss for a Bigger or Better Workspace

Icebreaker: I need to discuss a problem that I fear is affecting the quality of my work. I've grown out of my workspace. The lack of space for my files [or] the inability to meet with clients [or] the lack for space for a staff meeting is preventing me from working at maximum efficiency. It's getting increasingly frustrating, and I'd like to move to a larger space.

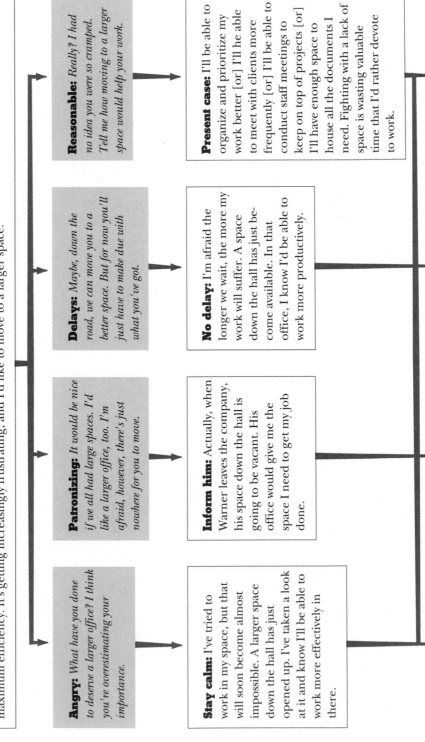

Angry: *What have you done to deserve a larger office? I think you're overestimating your importance.*

Stay calm: I've tried to work in my space, but that will soon become almost impossible. A larger space down the hall has just opened up. I've taken a look at it and know I'll be able to work more effectively in there.

Patronizing: *It would be nice if we all had large spaces. I'd like a larger office, too. I'm afraid, however, there's just nowhere for you to move.*

Inform him: Actually, when Warner leaves the company, his space down the hall is going to be vacant. His office would give me the space I need to get my job done.

Delays: *Maybe, down the road, we can move you to a better space. But for now you'll just have to make due with what you've got.*

No delay: I'm afraid the longer we wait, the more my work will suffer. A space down the hall has just become available. In that office, I know I'd be able to work more productively.

Reasonable: *Really? I had no idea you were so cramped. Tell me how moving to a larger space would help your work.*

Present case: I'll be able to organize and prioritize my work better [or] I'll be able to meet with clients more frequently [or] I'll be able to conduct staff meetings to keep on top of projects [or] I'll have enough space to house all the documents I need. Fighting with a lack of space is wasting valuable time that I'd rather devote to work.

No movement: *In the past, office upgrades have been done on a seniority or merit basis. If I make an exception for you, everyone will want a new office.*

Delays: *Is there a space open? Well, I still think we should hold off for a while. Other spaces will become available in the future. Just be patient and wait your turn.*

Confused: *I still don't understand what's wrong with the space you have now. You'll just have to make more room for yourself. Be a little creative.*

Agrees: *OK. I see your point. I don't see any reason why you shouldn't move. Let me talk to the people upstairs and get the OK from them.*

Not enough space: Believe me, I've tried many different ways of organizing the space and my work, but it's simply too small. There's just not enough room for my needs.

Convince him: I understand your position and past company policy, but I need the larger space for the benefit of my work, not my increased comfort. Because of that, I was hoping you'd consider my situation a priority.

No delay: I don't want to appear impatient, but I think this situation is reaching critical mass. If we wait any longer, my productivity may decline.

No: *Listen, you're not in line for a larger office, and I can't make an exception for you. You have to manage in your current space.*

Maybe: *OK. To be fair, I'll have to wait and see who else is going to request the new space. At the end of this week, I'll review all the requests and give it to the most deserving individual.*

Follow up: OK. That sounds fair. I'm going to write a quick memo outlining the reasons I need a larger space. I'll drop it off later today so you can look at it prior to making your decision. Thanks for discussing the matter with me.

Retreat and regroup: I understand. I'll do the best I can with the space I have and I'll look into other ways of making the space more workable. Perhaps we can meet again when the next larger space comes open. Thanks for meeting with me.

- **Preparation:** Search around the office and have specific spaces in mind prior to your meeting. Have examples of how your smaller space is negatively affecting your work and how a larger space will improve it.
- **Behavior:** Act worried. After all, if you don't get a larger space, your work will suffer. Your boss will recognize dedication and reward it.

ADAPTATIONS

This script can be modified to:
- Ask to share an office with a different person.
- Ask to move because of a problem coworker.

KEY POINTS

- Scout out available spaces within your company.
- Stress moving to a larger space is about work quality, not personal comfort or ego.
- Try to get an answer about moving soon—don't let your boss delay the situation.
- If he tells you he'll think about it and get back to you, prepare a memo so your points stay fresh in his mind.
- If he says no, don't panic. Tell him you'd like to be considered for the next open space.

Asking Your Boss for *12.*
Additional Responsibilities

STRATEGY

Approach this meeting like a job interview. Being eager is one thing, but being prepared is another. Work extra hard the weeks before this meeting. Demonstrate you can easily handle your current assignments. Recognize that asking for additional responsibilities will trigger a discussion of your employment history. Your boss will refer to every failure, no matter how insignificant. Be ready to respond with information about all your successes too, and to answer questions about past assignments. Still, try not to dwell on small episodes. Instead, make your boss focus on the big picture. Overall, you've done a good job and deserve more responsibility. Explain that you're happy with your job, but discouraged by a lack of challenges. Tell your boss that expanding your role at the office will save the company time and money. Present specific ideas for expanding your responsibilities. Refer to ongoing projects and display your knowledge of company policies and procedures. You have to prove your familiarity with the company and be interested in the work. If she denies your request initially, don't panic. Calmly defend your work record and, if necessary, compromise. You can suggest working as an assistant on a new project. This will expand your work portfolio and satisfy your boss as you ease into more responsibilities. Another tactic is offering to take work on a trial basis. Suggest a month of new responsibilities, after which you and your boss can meet to discuss your performance and progress. Identify your boss's particular concern and address it head on— you'll be rewarded with more to do.

TACTICS

- **Attitude:** Be confident and enthusiastic. You're displaying a strong work ethic, something an employer loves to see. Make your boss understand your need for more responsibility.
- **Timing:** Schedule this meeting following some type of personal success. Your boss will have your most recent work in mind during the conversation, so it's important this meeting follow a job well done.
- **Preparation:** Try to learn everything and anything you can about the company. Show off your knowledge during the meeting. Your goal is to impress your boss with your interest in the company's projects.
- **Behavior:** Stay calm no matter what negatives from your past are dredged up. Steer your boss toward a discussion of job performance. When speaking, don't be afraid to show your passion for your job.

47

12. Asking Your Boss for Additional Responsibilities

Icebreaker and pitch: I really enjoy my job and feel I've learned a lot working here. I believe I've shown a firm grasp of my assignments and dedication to my job. With that in mind, I'd like to take on more responsibilities, branch out, and contribute more. I'm comfortable with my workload and will have no problem taking on more work.

Not ready: *You fell pretty far behind on the spring report, remember? I think you need to work on certain skills before we entrust you with extra responsibilities.*

Delay: *I think you're getting a little bit ahead of yourself. You're doing a good job, but I think you need more experience in your current role. Just be patient.*

Wait your turn: *We have a full staff on every project. I know it seems like you've been working on the same type of assignments for a while, but you're too valuable where you are now to be moved. I need everyone to be a team player.*

Yes: *I'm glad you came to me. It's good to see someone taking an aggressive interest in work. What kind of responsibilities were you thinking about?*

Big picture: I realize I was behind on the spring report, but I worked hard and did make the deadline. Overall, I think my record speaks for itself. I'm dedicated to my job, and I'd really like to become more involved.

Now: I understand what you're saying, but I'm ready for a new challenge. I'd like the opportunity to prove how much more I can do. I just want to help the company and contribute to its success.

Make room: I won't abandon my current responsibilities. I just want to expand my role. Being involved on the fall update would allow me to be part of a large project, meet tough deadlines, and broaden my skills as an employee.

Plan: I'd like an expanded role on the fall update. There are some available assignments I can handle. Given the opportunity, I can help insure we deliver the update on time.

Disagrees: *I appreciated your hard work, but you still fell behind. If you give a full effort over the next quarter we can discuss giving you extra work. Until then you need to prove yourself to me.*

Too risky: *I'm not sure I can risk spreading you too thin. If we assign you extra work, your current assignment may suffer. It's just not the time for us to be taking chances.*

Maybe: *Well, I'm not sure how comfortable I am giving you more work. It may confuse your priorities and cause more problems than it solves.*

OK: *It's true we need an extra hand on the fall project. It would be a big help, but do you have enough time for all that work? I don't want you biting off more than you can chew.*

Alternative: What about assigning work on a trial basis? You can give me a couple of extra assignments and let me give it my best shot. After a month, you and I can meet again and evaluate my performance.

Compromise: Well, I know Ms. Ward has her hands full with marketing. What if I help her out a few hours a week? It wouldn't be a full time commitment, but I would still be contributing and expanding my role.

You're ready: I've given this serious thought, and I'm certain I can handle more work. I've researched the goals of the fall project and know exactly where I can contribute. I hope you'll give me a chance to pitch in and help the company.

Reschedule: Perhaps we can meet again in a couple of months to discuss this further. It would give me a goal to work toward. If it's all right with you, I'll schedule another meeting with your assistant.

No: *I admire your desire to help, but I think it's just too soon for you to take on more work. Maybe down the road we can discuss it, but for now I have to say no.*

Yes: *All right, you convinced me. We'll meet next week and talk about your role on the fall project. You've been doing good work—I'll expect more of the same.*

Agrees: *That sounds like a reasonable solution. We'll try your suggestion and see how it works out. You'll be responsible for your old and new assignments. If I see a decline in work quality, I'll have to withdraw your new responsibilities.*

Express gratitude: Thank you for the opportunity and your confidence in me. I look forward to our meeting and starting work on the fall update.

ADAPTATIONS

This script can be modified to:

- Request work with a new client or customer.
- Offer your services for an experimental or new project.

KEY POINTS

- If your work record is questioned, calmly defend your actions and quickly refocus the conversation on your entire employment history.
- Express a strong desire to expand your work horizons and help the company.
- Have in mind a specific assignment or project on which you'd like to work.
- If you meet resistance, suggest a compromise or alternative.
- If your boss refuses, schedule a follow-up meeting and try again.

Breaking Bad News to Your Boss

13.

STRATEGY

This is one of the most stressful and difficult dialogues you could have with a superior. Not only are you somewhat embarrassed by the failure—whether it was your fault or not—but you're also worried the setback could affect your standing in the organization. The key to fulfilling your obligations and minimizing any potential damage to you is to turn this meeting as quickly as possible into a discussion about what to do now, rather than a postmortem of what went wrong. The secrets of doing that are to make sure the news comes from you so you can control the spin; demonstrate that the situation was beyond your control or accept the responsibility; and present a plan of action that mitigates the damage.

TACTICS

- **Attitude:** Approach this as an opportunity to prove you're resourceful and can take charge in a crisis. Be willing to accept the responsibility for what has happened, but not necessarily the blame. Finally, realize that your supervisor's anger may not be at you, but with the situation.
- **Preparation:** Have an explanation for why the problem has occurred. If there were any hints of trouble, be ready to explain what you did in response. Most importantly, have a detailed written proposal that suggests a course of action.
- **Timing:** While you shouldn't burst into a closed-door meeting and blurt out the news, you must bring this to your supervisor's attention as soon as you can. It's essential the news comes from you first.
- **Behavior:** Don't show contrition unless you are actually to blame. However, do show concern, not for yourself, but for the company. Use every possible chance to move beyond what happened to what to do now. Don't shy away from playing to your supervisor's ego, but try to be subtle. Sucking up won't take the place of accepting responsibility, but it can help deflect free-floating anger.

13. Breaking Bad News to Your Boss

Icebreaker: I have some bad news. Although I think we'll be OK in the long run, Bill Smith from Acme just called to tell me they're moving to the L&H Agency.

Demonstrate you're blameless: He emphasized that they've had no problems with our work—it was strictly a dollars-and-cents move. You were right when you said they were looking for million-dollar results on a hundred-dollar budget.

Acknowledge some responsibility: They'd raised some concerns about our approach, but I was addressing them. They just jumped the gun on me. You were right when you warned me that Acme is very impatient for results.

Calm response: *They're one of our biggest accounts. They've been with us for five years. What happened?*

Disbelieving response: *Acme has been with us for five years. Now they walk out with no warning, and you think your handling of the account had nothing to do with it?*

Angry response: *I can't believe you screwed this up. I don't know what I was thinking when I let you take over Acme. Do you know how much this will cost us?*

Threatening response: *If I can't trust you to handle Acme, maybe you can't handle Apex either. And with this happening, I wouldn't count on a raise any time soon.*

Take charge: I think the general slowdown in the industry was the straw that broke the camel's back. Even though we did everything possible, I take full responsibility for what happened and for replacing the lost revenue. I've come up with a plan I think will work.

Absorb anger: I understand your anger; I'm upset, too, even though I believe we were on the right track. I know how important this account is to us, and I've come up with a plan that I think can replace, maybe even top, what we earn on the Acme account.

Receptive response: *I'm open to suggestions. We certainly can't afford to lose that amount of revenue.*

Skeptical response: *I'd like to hear it, although I don't see how we can replace a client of such long standing that easily.*

Political response: *First, think about how we're going to break the news to the people upstairs. They're going to want heads to roll.*

Present the plan: I've drawn up this list of possible replacements for Acme, all of which should bring in at least as much business as it has, possibly more. That should reassure the folks upstairs about the way we're handling the situation. But I don't think we should give up on Acme just yet. I know we can get them to meet with us. And I think with you there, we'd have a great chance to win them back.

ADAPTATIONS

This script can be modified to:
- Break bad news to parents, friends, spouses, teachers, and others.
- Deliver negative financial news to an investor or partner.

KEY POINTS

- Be direct, but try to offer some hope as soon as possible.
- Demonstrate immediately you're blameless or acknowledge your responsibility.
- If your supervisor takes the news well, or still questions your account, restate your position and move right on to your plan of action.
- If your supervisor gets angry or threatens you, try to get on his side by saying you're angry too, and then move on to what you think should be done now.
- Whatever the initial response to your plan, reaffirm your belief that it will work, add some flattery, and offer whatever help you can in overcoming the problem.

Dealing with a Performance Review by Your Boss

14.

STRATEGY

The key to getting the most from a positive performance review, or minimizing the damage from a negative one, is to subtly take charge of the conversation by preempting the reviewer. If you expect a positive review, immediately launch into the new challenges you'd like to take on. If you expect a negative review, immediately describe your plan to improve. The idea is to get off the negative-issues discussion as quickly as possible and turn this meeting into a positive and constructive outline of your plan. If you don't succeed in taking control, push for a subsequent meeting and try again.

TACTICS

- **Attitude:** Look on this as a chance to take charge of your future, rather than as a postmortem on your past.
- **Preparation:** Conduct a thorough self-analysis to determine whether your review will be primarily positive or negative. Then, develop a plan to either take advantage of the positive review or correct past mistakes and shortcomings.
- **Timing:** While you'll have little control over when this meeting takes place, be ready to postpone it should anything problematic occur during the conversation. For example, if you're in your supervisor's office discussing your performance, and she gets a call that the company's largest customer has gone bankrupt, immediately suggest an adjournment.
- **Behavior:** When receiving constructive criticism or compliments, it's important to acknowledge them with more than just physical gestures. Rather than just nodding, say you understand. Take your supervisor's suggestions, put them in your own words, and repeat them. Offer sincere thanks for any input, positive or negative.

14. Dealing with a Performance Review by Your Boss

Expect positive review: I believe I've met most of last year's goals—I've brought in new clients and revamped our marketing strategy. So I've developed some new goals I'd like to shoot for.

Expect negative review: I know that I've had some difficulties this year and that some clients have complained. I've thought a lot about what happened and why, and about how I can improve.

Icebreaker: I really enjoy my work, so I'm glad to have this opportunity to talk with you.

Gives up control: *I've been very happy with your work, and I'm pleased that you took those goals so seriously. What do you have in mind for next year?*

Retains control: *In general, you've done a very good job this year, but there are a few areas I think you need to work on. [Explains specifics.]*

Gives up control: *I haven't been pleased with your performance, and I'm glad you realize that. Now tell me what you plan to do to turn things around.*

Retains control: *I have gotten negative feedback, and that has added to my own concerns. Let me tell you what I see as the major problems. [Explains specifics.]*

Defense: I think I was so focused on drumming up new business that I neglected some of our existing clients. So I've started taking clients out and mending fences.

Your pitch: I've enjoyed working in marketing, but I think I'd be more useful if I had financial expertise, too. So I'd like to take on budgeting.

Lead-in to pitch: [After hearing and repeating specifics] I appreciate your suggestions, and I'll work hard on them. I'd also like to get your feedback on my idea.

Lead-in to defense: [After hearing and repeating specifics] I understand completely, and I'll get right on it. In fact, I've already started to address some problems.

Accepts pitch: *That's a great idea. Why don't you start by tackling ways to cut costs in your own department.*

Rejects pitch: *I'm not sure you're ready for the added responsibilities. I'd like you to focus on marketing a while longer.*

Push for another meeting: I understand, and I'll give it my best. But can we schedule another meeting three months from now, when we could talk again about other ways I can contribute?

Accepts defense: *I'm glad you've started to work on these problems. If you follow through, things should work out.*

Rejects defense: *You'll have to do a lot more than make nice with a few clients to get back on track.*

Push for another meeting: I understand, and I'll start working on the problems right away. Could you review my performance again in, say, three months, and let me know if I'm on the right track?

ADAPTATIONS

This script can be modified to:

- Counter a problem that may arise when you're discussing a proposed raise or promotion.
- Use as a segue into a discussion of a raise or promotion.

KEY POINTS

- Stress how much you love your job and that you've looked forward to this meeting—whether it's true or not.
- If you expect a positive review, immediately launch into what you'd like to do in the coming year in order to set up raise or promotion discussions.
- If you expect a negative review, admit your problems and immediately launch into your plan for self-improvement.
- If your supervisor doesn't let you take charge of the conversation, segue into your plan after absorbing his comments.
- If your supervisor doesn't accept your plan, ask for another meeting at which you can try to take charge once again.

Justifying a Questionable Expense Report

15.

STRATEGY

You need to tread very carefully if one of your expense reports is questioned by a supervisor. You can assume that if you're called into a face-to-face meeting, the problem isn't one of documentation—that could be handled with a telephone call or a visit from an administrative assistant or bookkeeper. Therefore, this meeting is calling into question either your judgment or your honesty. It's even possible there's a hidden agenda—perhaps your supervisor is building a case for termination or for a negative review. Whatever the situation, your goal is to immediately admit to the error, but turn it into one of omission rather than commission. Your mistake was not catching the error yourself or not preparing management for the unusual charge.

TACTICS

- **Attitude:** Take this as a very serious probe, even if it's for a small amount. You need to clearly demonstrate that this in no way reflects on your honesty or judgment.
- **Preparation:** Unless you're given advance notice of a problem with your report you'll have little or no time to prepare for this specific meeting. Instead, make it your business always to double- and triple-check your expense reports prior to submission and *never* to knowingly pad them.
- **Timing:** You'll also have no control over the timing of this meeting. The only element of timing you can control is to have an immediate answer ready for any questions: Either the questionable expense was a mistake or you forgot to provide advance warning.
- **Behavior:** Even though this may be a probe of your personal integrity, don't become defensive. And never, ever argue, no matter what the amount involved; the risk is too great. Anger is a defense mechanism. It could be seen as an admission of guilt and could turn the meeting into a confrontation rather than a conversation. Instead, be forthright, sincere, and if need be, apologetic.

15. Justifying a Questionable Expense Report

Opener: *I have a problem with your expense report for last week's trip to Las Vegas.*

Express puzzled concern: Is there a problem with my documentation?

You spent too much: *No, your documentation is fine. The problem is how much you spent. Don't you think $600 for a dinner for four is way out of line?*

Personal, not business: *No, your documentation is fine. The problem is you've got about $100 here for in-room movies. It's not our obligation to pay for your entertainment when you're not out with clients.*

Not your choice: You're absolutely right. But I left the choice of restaurants up to them. Since I initiated the dinner, and they're such good clients, I felt I had no choice but to pick up the check. If you look at past reports, you'll see I usually take clients to Joe's, where the prices are more reasonable. I really felt dreadful for the company. I'm sorry—I should have attached a note explaining the situation.

It was a mistake: I'm sorry. I didn't realize that was on the bill. Normally I [or] my secretary audit the hotel bills before submitting them, but I used the rapid checkout and didn't have a chance this time. I never intended the company to have to pay for those charges. I'll take care of it right away. It won't happen again.

Question explanation: *That sounds like a reasonable explanation. But what if I hadn't gone over your bill so closely—what would've happened then?*

Wants more notice: *I understand. In the future, just remember I have to send these upstairs. I need some warning if there's anything unusual so I can offer my own explanations.*

Reaffirm honesty: The minute I saw the mistake, I would've reimbursed the company for the personal charges, whether or not they were discovered.

Express thanks: Thanks for being so understanding. I appreciate it. It won't happen again.

ADAPTATIONS

This script can be modified to:
- Explain a financial surprise to a spouse or partner.
- Explain an error in an employment, loan, or credit application.

KEY POINTS

- Even though you know it's not likely, ask if the problem is with your documentation. This shows you're feeling no guilt and were unaware of any potential problems.
- If you're accused of requesting reimbursement for personal expenses, immediately explain that the inclusion of the charges on your report was a mistake.
- If you're accused of spending too much, show how the cost was beyond your control and admit that it was a mistake not to provide forewarning of the unusually large charge.
- If your explanation is questioned, reaffirm your honesty as strongly as possible.
- Always express your thanks and stress the mistake won't happen again.

Asking Your Boss to Deal with a Problem Peer

16.

STRATEGY

Your boss is only interested in what affects work production. If your problem with a peer is a personal dislike, difference of opinion, or other nonproduction-related matter, she won't care, nor should she. In order to get her involved, you need to demonstrate that the problem is affecting your efficiency or that of your department. Make your approach only after trying all you can to resolve the situation on your own. If your boss remains reluctant to get involved, even after you demonstrate that the problem is influencing work, stress that you've run out of other options. If you can't get her to intervene, agree to make one final effort at solving the matter on your own, but only if she agrees to intervene if you're unsuccessful. Try to insure the situation doesn't have a negative impact on your reputation. You don't want to be perceived as a whiner or a rat, you just want to be able to do your job. The more you show the boss your main concern is the company, not yourself, the better chance she'll help you resolve the problem.

TACTICS

- **Attitude:** Be remorseful, but not apologetic. It's a shame the situation has reached this point, but it's not your fault. Remember: Work is suffering because of the problem and you've tried everything you can on your own.
- **Timing:** Approach your boss only after you've truly made every possible effort to independently solve the problem. At the same time, don't wait until the problem significantly damages your production.
- **Preparation:** Develop a concise description of the problem, as well as a list of your varied failed attempts at solving it on your own.
- **Behavior:** Be worried about the quality of your work. You simply want to be able to work without unnecessary interference. Your boss will appreciate concern for the company.

16. Asking Your Boss to Deal with a Problem Peer

Icebreaker: I'd like to talk with you about a problem that's affecting my work. Charlene is consistently demeaning me in front of clients. I've tried on numerous occasions to speak with her and resolve the problem, but my attempts have been unsuccessful. I believe you're the only person who can make her understand the severity of the situation. I need your help.

Upset: *I'm glad you came to me. I won't tolerate that kind of behavior. Why didn't you come to me sooner?*

Explain problem: Well, recently the problem has escalated and I feel it's time for you to intervene. Completing my assignments successfully is becoming nearly impossible and her behavior could definitely hurt the company's image and reputation.

Mildly interested: *Well, if she's affecting your work or damaging the company's reputation or image, that's unacceptable. Still, I'd like to see you try to solve this problem without my help. You can't give up every time you run into a little resistance.*

Need help: I wouldn't come to you unless I believed the problem was beyond my power. I've tried everything, but nothing has changed. My work is starting to be affected, and I fear that, without attention, the problem will grow.

Not interested: *I really don't have the time for this. You and Charlene will have to come to a mutual understanding; I'm not a den mother. Try to solve the problem yourself.*

Emphasize the problem: I've tried countless times to get through to her, but nothing I've done has worked. The only option left is for you to speak with her. I'm concerned this problem will not only throw me off schedule, but will harm the company's reputation.

Agrees: *You're probably right. I can speak with Charlene directly and see what she has to say. Do you have any ideas about how to approach her?*

Ideas: Charlene needs to realize that her behavior is undermining me and the company, and is turning off clients.

Coming around: *Well, I guess I see your point. Before I get involved, I'd like you to talk with Charlene so she won't feel ambushed. Tell her we spoke and see if her behavior changes for the better. I'd like you both to arrive at a solution without my interference.*

Agrees to alternative: *OK. If you speak with Charlene and the problem persists, I'll meet with her and straighten things out.*

Still unmoved: *I've heard these kind of complaints before. I'll keep an eye on Charlene, but I really don't want to get involved in a personal dispute. I would much prefer if the two of you settled this matter.*

Alternative: I'll speak with Charlene and give it one more try. However, if that fails, I'd like to count on your involvement. I'm afraid if we wait too long, the problem will grow beyond repair.

ADAPTATIONS

This script can be modified to:

- Ask a superior to speak with a problem client.
- Ask a supervisor to speak with a problem customer.

KEY POINTS

- The problem has to affect your work and the company for your boss to get involved.
- Emphasize that you've tried to solve the problem on your own many times, but have failed.
- Give examples of how the problem is hindering your work.
- If your boss insists you try again on your own, ask for an assurance she will intervene if you fail once more.

Tattling on a Peer to Your Boss

17

STRATEGY

Deciding whether to complain about a peer's performance is a tough call. Even if your gripes are entirely justified and your boss supports you, you can end up being viewed as a back stabber. So pick your fights carefully. If someone simply rubs you the wrong way, that's your problem. The only time it's worth entering these dangerous waters is when someone's sloppy work or procrastination is jeopardizing your ability to get your job done, and you've already tried unsuccessfully to set things right (see Lifescripts 40 and 41). Your goal in this script is to enlist your boss's direct intervention without incurring criticism yourself. You want to minimize any damage to your reputation and avoid being labeled the boss's spy. You can accomplish all this as long as you stress the connection to your own productivity and the company's goals. Make it clear that this is an unusual situation, not your common practice.

TACTICS

- **Attitude:** Your first loyalty must be to the company. It's by following this credo that you'll achieve your own success. You aren't putting someone down to boost yourself—you're helping the company achieve its goals.
- **Preparation:** Make sure you've established what you feel is the problem—quality or delay, for instance—and that you've tried on your own to resolve the situation.
- **Timing:** The timing here is tricky. You want to wait long enough so that action is vital, but not so long that it's a crisis beyond repair.
- **Behavior:** Show remorse at having to take this step, but offer no apologies. You have the company's goals at heart and there's no shame in that.

17. Tattling on a Peer to Your Boss

Icebreaker: Excuse me, Alan, but I need to speak with you. I'm afraid there's a problem with meeting our deadline for the Oxford proposal [or] I'm afraid the Oxford proposal just isn't going to meet our usual standards. I've asked several times, but David has yet to turn in his final sketches for the project [or] The sketches I've gotten from David just aren't up to par.

Wants to hear: *You know how important that project is. I'm not going to let anything keep us from delivering the kind of work we promised, and delivering it on time. What exactly is the problem?*

Upset at idea: *Listen, that project is crucial. I made you the lead person on it, and I don't want to hear any excuses or buck passing. Your job—and his—is to get it done right, and on time.*

Offer reassurance: I understand your concern, and I'm sure we'll meet the deadline if we solve this problem now. But I really need your help. Without it, I don't think I'll be able to get what we need out of David.

Insists on your involvement: *Okay, you go back to David and tell him that you spoke with me and I said he'd better shape up. Let me know how it goes.*

Not doing work: I know David is under a lot of pressure—we all are. But I'm not sure he has even begun the sketches I need from him. I've asked for them repeatedly, but he hasn't delivered. And we're running out of time.

Work not up to par: I know David is under a lot of pressure—we all are. But the sketches he has given me just aren't the quality we need. We've spoken about it repeatedly, but there's been no improvement. And we're running out of time.

Against ratting: *I'll make sure he delivers. But please remember, teamwork is important. I'm not happy about your coming here and complaining about a colleague.*

Wants more dirt: *Have you had problems with David in the past? What do you think of the job he and the rest of his people are doing overall?*

Deflect probe for info: I really can't give you a general evaluation. I'm not familiar with the work he has done for and with others.

Deflect criticism: Teamwork is important to me, too. But so is making sure we get the job done. If I had made headway with him, I wouldn't have brought it up.

Argue for reconsideration: All right, I'll give it one last try. But if it doesn't produce the results we want, can I count on your help at that point?

Accepts responsibility: *OK. I'll speak with him, find out what the problem is, and make sure you get the sketches on time.*

Agrees to act later: *Deal. If you really can't get him in line by the end of next week, come back, give me an update, and I'll get involved directly.*

ADAPTATIONS

This script can be modified to:

- Speak to a customer or supplier about the behavior of one of his employees.
- Speak to a partner at a professional firm you associate with about the behavior of another partner.
- Speak to a store manager about a clerk's behavior.
- Speak to a principal about your child's teacher.

KEY POINTS

- Be clear about the problem and present it entirely in business terms.
- If your boss initially objects to getting involved, insist that you need him in order to get the job done.
- If your boss probes for more information on your colleague, stress that you have none to offer and that your concern is this project.
- If he insists on staying aloof, ask for a commitment that he'll get involved if you're once again unsuccessful.
- If he criticizes your coming to him with complaints about a peer, stress that you've only done it because the project was in jeopardy.

Asking Your Boss to Stop Harassing You

18.

STRATEGY

You've landed a good job and hopped on the career track, and all of a sudden your immediate superior threatens to derail your dreams. She's criticizing you constantly, usually in the presence of coworkers; she's using foul language; or she's just downright rude. You need to find out why—and ask her to cease and desist. But this is a narrow track you must walk with caution. Be too passive and apologetic, and you risk not being taken seriously. Be too aggressive and accusatory, and you risk stepping on the third rail and losing your job. The right mix of assurance and rationality should let your boss see the error of her ways. If not, don't jump off the trestle; if need be, you can go over your boss's head.

TACTICS

- **Attitude:** Be calm, nonconfrontational, and unapologetic. You want to set the example here. It's likely your boss will react angrily, so be prepared to absorb that and go on. Present your case rationally and coolly.
- **Preparation:** Have specific examples of the abuse in hand. Document her bad behavior outlining date, time, situation, what was said, and who was present. Be prepared to present this information.
- **Timing:** Again, set the example. Ask your boss for a good time to meet in her office, or if that's not possible, somewhere private. Make sure to have this meeting as soon as possible after an outburst.
- **Behavior:** You want to keep this job, so make sure your dedication is apparent. But don't downplay the seriousness of your predicament—your boss needs to know you feel you're being unfairly treated, and if need be, you will go over her head. Remember your focus is professional, not personal. Don't let this encounter deteriorate into a name-calling free-for-all; this isn't a talk show, it's your career. Keep it short and sweet.

18. Asking Your Boss to Stop Harassing You

Icebreaker: Thanks for taking the time to meet with me, Ms. Gates. I think we need to discuss your feelings regarding my job performance. For some time now, I've sensed your displeasure with my work and abilities. And to be perfectly honest, I feel it's unwarranted. I'm not opposed to honest discussions of my performance, I would just prefer that they take place in private, away from coworkers. I'd like to know what we can do to correct this.

Accepting/open to discussion: *Ms. Bloom, I really had no idea you felt this way. You're one of the best young people in the department, so perhaps I do tend to push you a little harder. I'll try to keep it in check. I appreciate your candor. Keep up the good work.*

Denies the problem: *Really, Ms. Bloom, don't you think you're being a little hypersensitive? If you want to make it in this business, you're going to have to learn how to take some constructive criticism from a supervisor. You know what they say, "If you can't take the heat..."*

Reacts angrily: Is that right? *You feel I'm being too hard on you? Jeez, I knew you'd be trouble the moment you were hired. I said to myself, "Watch your back, Betty. There's someone who's only out for number one." I was right. Maybe if you spent less time making these kinds of ridiculous accusations, you might actually get some work done.*

Calmly restate problem: No, Ms. Gates, I don't think so. I know the difference between constructive criticism and inappropriate remarks. I'm a good worker, and I'd like to get better, so I would appreciate any help you could give, but I feel the things you've said are more insult than insight. I would really like to know what we can do to change this.

Offer thanks: Thanks, Ms. Gates, I will.

Accepts/apologizes: *I honestly didn't see that this was a problem. I'm sorry if you felt this way, but I'm sorry if I was rude—I've got a lot of pressure from above, too, and I guess I take it out on the staff sometimes.*

Still in denial: *Really, Ms. Bloom, I'm sorry you feel this way, but I think maybe this is your problem, not mine.*

Remains angry: *I don't know who you think you are, or who you think you're dealing with, but this is a ridiculous waste of my time. Are you paranoid or something? Maybe you need professional help. You'll never get anywhere in this company, that's for damn sure.*

Close the issue: I'm sorry you see this as an attack, Ms. Gates. I came to see you because I thought we could discuss this rationally. I didn't want it to come to this, but based on this conversation, I feel it's necessary to for me to speak with Ms. Diver. [See Lifescript 19: Going over your boss's head.]

ADAPTATIONS

This script can be modified to:

- Ask a family member or friend to stop harassing you.

KEY POINTS

- Calm rationality is key. Present your case honestly and unapologetically. Coming on too strong may hurt your chance to solve the problem.
- Don't be surprised at anger. An insecure boss might see this as a play for power. Relax, stay your course, and tell your boss you're willing to go higher for help.
- Should your assertions meet with apology and/or acceptance, let your boss know that you appreciate her honesty and willingness to help.
- In the event that anger and/or denial don't subside, stay firm. Reassert your position and state your intention to go over her head. Remember to document this meeting as well.
- Don't be pulled into an argument over smaller or personal issues.

Going Over Your Boss's Head

19.

STRATEGY

Taking a problem to your boss's boss is one of the biggest gambles in office politics. The payoff can be great, but you run the risk of becoming a pariah whose days in the company are numbered. That's why you should take this step only if you believe your future at the firm is at stake—because of a negative performance review, say, or because a vital project has been canceled. First, try to get permission for your maneuver. You may get the OK if you frame your request as a search for expert input. Even if your immediate boss objects, persevere. Asking to go over his head is as bad as actually doing it, so you've nothing more to lose. When you do get upstairs, continue to frame your efforts as a search for advice. Resist the temptation to bad-mouth your boss. If you manage to win the top person over, you'll have gained a valuable ally—one who will most likely be able to protect you from recriminations. If you don't win Mr. Big to your side, start looking for another job.

TACTICS

- **Attitude:** Realize there's nothing your immediate boss can do to stop you, but you'd still like his permission.
- **Preparation:** Have your facts and arguments down cold—your future in the company will depend on your winning your boss's boss over to your side.
- **Timing:** While this should be done soon after either a negative review or the cancellation of an important project, your decision must be thought out, not reflexive. Give yourself at least a day or two to think things over.
- **Behavior:** Be forthright and determined. You must convey that you're bucking the system because of your extremely principled position and concern for justice.

19. Going Over Your Boss's Head

Project icebreaker—boss: I understand your objections to the project. Would you have a problem if I unofficially batted this around with Steven? Maybe he can help us come up with a way to overcome your objections.

Personal icebreaker—boss: Thanks for your time. I have a request. I'd like permission to speak with Steven about [the issue under dispute].

No need: *I've already spoken to Steven. He's in accord with me.*

New spin: I'd assumed you had, but I think I can put another spin on it that might change both of your minds.

No permission: *You can do whatever you want, but you don't have my permission.*

Refuses: *I don't want you speaking to anyone else about this.*

Won't help: *This is my decision to make. Speaking to Steven won't change my mind.*

Still want to: That may be the case, but I don't want to do it without first letting you know. I'd like your permission to try.

Express thanks: : Thank you. I appreciate it [or] Thanks for your time.

Am I forbidden?: Are you saying if the issue comes up I should say you've forbidden me to discuss it?

Grudging permission: : If you want to waste your time, it's OK with me.

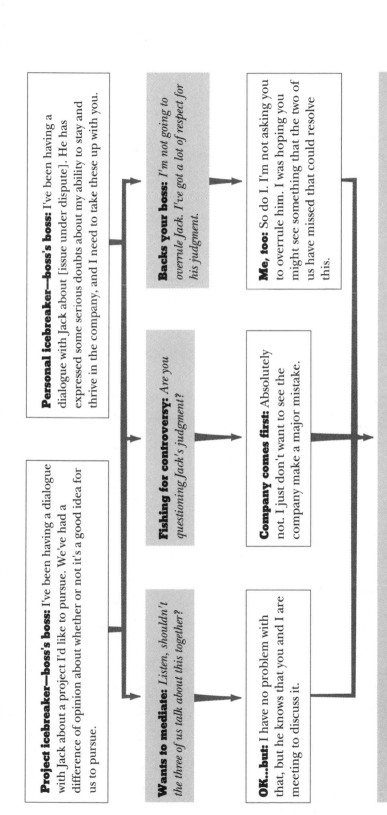

Project icebreaker—boss's boss: I've been having a dialogue with Jack about a project I'd like to pursue. We've had a difference of opinion about whether or not it's a good idea for us to pursue.

Personal icebreaker—boss's boss: I've been having a dialogue with Jack about [issue under dispute]. He has expressed some serious doubts about my ability to stay and thrive in the company, and I need to take these up with you.

Wants to mediate: *Listen, shouldn't the three of us talk about this together?*

Fishing for controversy: *Are you questioning Jack's judgment?*

Backs your boss: *I'm not going to overrule Jack. I've got a lot of respect for his judgment.*

OK..but: I have no problem with that, but he knows that you and I are meeting to discuss it.

Company comes first: Absolutely not. I just don't want to see the company make a major mistake.

Me, too: So do I. I'm not asking you to overrule him. I was hoping you might see something that the two of us have missed that could resolve this.

Agrees to intervene: *OK. Tell me about the project [or] Tell me about the situation.*

ADAPTATIONS

This script can be modified to:
- Appeal a loan rejection.
- Correct detrimental or incorrect information your boss has passed along to his boss.

KEY POINTS

- Frame your jumping the ladder as a search for expert advice.
- If your immediate boss objects, persist.
- Regardless of your immediate boss's conclusion, thank him.
- If your boss's boss wants to serve as mediator, explain that your immediate boss knows of this meeting.
- If your boss's boss fishes for controversy, stress that your concern is first and foremost for the company.
- If your boss's boss refuses to overrule a decision, stress you're looking for a potential compromise, not a reversal.

Giving Notice to Your Boss

20.

STRATEGY

Giving notice can be dangerous, even when you already have another job. It's conceivable an angry boss could fire you on the spot, forcing you to lose at least two weeks' pay. If you give too much notice, you could end up getting fired as soon as you've wrapped up your work or your replacement is selected. The solution is to give the two weeks that have become customary, and to be prepared to deflect attempts to fire you. The best way to do that is to practice a subtle form of workplace extortion. Your obligation to conclude short-term projects and prepare memos on your long-term projects should be implicit with your being given two weeks to wrap things up. By the way, it makes sense to hold off actually preparing and presenting those memos as long as possible, because they're your only leverage to ensure that you get your final paycheck.

TACTICS

- **Attitude:** Be direct, businesslike, and confident. The only thing she can do to you is fire you—and you're leaving for another job anyway.
- **Preparation:** In this script it's actually more a matter of not preparing. State what you'll do during your two weeks as a lame duck, but don't actually do it until you've gotten her agreement that you'll be employed for those two weeks.
- **Timing:** Do this as soon as possible after learning you've been hired and have cleaned up your files. Do it as early in the day and as early in the week as possible, so the company has a chance to react right away.
- **Behavior:** Remain calm, even in the face of anger or threats. Don't simply absorb abuse, however. Make it clear that your being fired will not only hurt the company and the staff, but will send a clear message to other staff members that they should simply quit rather than give notice.

20. Giving Notice to Your Boss

Icebreaker: I've received an irresistible job offer from Acme, Inc., that I've accepted, effective two weeks from today. I've gone over everything that I'm working on here, and I believe that I'll be able to complete all of my short-term projects without incident or additional expense within two weeks. I'll prepare memos for those who take over my long-term projects.

Gets angry: *You ungrateful witch. We don't need your help. Pack up your stuff and get out of here today. And don't even try to take any of our customers. I'm going to call security right now and have them watch while you empty out your desk.*

Not enough time: *Two weeks' notice is like quitting on the spot. If that's all you can give me, you might as well leave today.*

Accepts inevitable: *I hate to see you go, but that's part of business. Just make sure you finish your projects and get those memos to me as soon as possible.*

Notice a mistake?: Was it a mistake to give you notice? Would you have preferred that I just leave? Is that how you want this company to operate? It's your choice. I've told everyone in my department that I'm leaving and that I'll help them with the transition. But if you want me to leave today without helping them, and you want everyone in the company to see it's a mistake to give you any notice at all, that's fine, too.

As much as possible: I honestly have considered your needs very carefully. As I said, I'll wrap up my short-term projects and prepare memos on my long-term assignments. I'll also do whatever I can to help you find a replacement for me. Finally, if necessary, I'll be available on weekends and evenings to help out my replacement, even after I make the shift. However, if you prefer that I leave today, I will.

Thanks: Thank you. I'll get those memos to you right away. Incidentally, working for you has been a real learning experience for me, and I'm grateful.

Backs off, some: *No, you can spend the next two weeks tying up loose ends. I should have realized I couldn't count on you. Get those memos to me as soon as possible.*

Backs off: *No. I was just worried about the workload. I'd appreciate your doing everything possible to get your work done. And get me those memos as soon as you can.*

ADAPTATIONS

This script can be modified to:

- Terminate a nonbusiness relationship.

KEY POINTS

- Be confident, direct, and determined. The die has been cast, so be forceful.
- If she gets angry and threatens to fire you, say that that will hurt the company and give the wrong message to employees.
- If she says two weeks isn't enough, tell her you'll do everything possible to help, but insist it's the best you can do.
- Unless she accepts the situation gracefully, give her the last word—it will help assuage her bruised ego.

Asking Your Boss for a Job Recommendation

21.

STRATEGY

Asking your current supervisor for a job recommendation can be extremely dangerous. Make sure that a job offer is assured from the company that seeks this recommendation, because the moment you tell him you're a candidate for another job, he mentally starts replacing you. And at the same time, he may be able to sabotage your future position. The objective of this script is to minimize his anger at you and ensure he'll put in a good word—or at least won't put in a bad word—with your future employer.

TACTICS

- **Attitude:** Don't look on this as asking for a favor or help. That makes it seem a big deal and gives him more of an opportunity to withhold his recommendation. You're simply asking for a professional courtesy— that's very difficult to withhold. Also, if he seems remote, you want nothing but the truth. Be aware that employers must be very careful about what they say about you since you could sue them if you don't get the job because of something they say or don't say.
- **Preparation:** Before having this conversation, you need to be able to put your finger on an inarguable reason for taking the job—something the new job offers that your current job can never provide. You also need to be prepared to say how long you'll be able to stick around.
- **Timing:** Because of the danger involved in this script, you need to wait until you're sure the only remaining hurdle to your getting the new job is a positive reference from your current employer. Of course, that means surprising your current supervisor, but you've really no choice.
- **Behavior:** The more you frame this as an unsolicited offer that you simply cannot refuse—and which no one who truly has your best interests at heart would advise you to refuse—the more likely you are to avoid a problem.

21. Asking Your Boss for a Job Recommendation

Icebreaker: I need to talk to you about some news I've just gotten. I've been given an incredible job offer—an opportunity I can't pass up. I've given your name as my most important reference because working with you has meant a tremendous amount to me. I'd really appreciate it if you would speak with them.

Accepting: *Look, as long as I get enough time to find your replacement, I'm happy for you.*

Reassure: I've told them you were both my mentor and my friend, and that I'd need to give you as much time as you need. They're eager to talk to you. I'd like your help.

You're making mistake: *I think you're making a mistake. You've got a wonderful future here. Are you sure you want to give it all up?*

Not really: I've had a wonderful career here, but this offers me [something current job can't], and we both know I could never get that here. That's why I need your help.

Goes ballistic: *You ungrateful SOB. This company has trained you, put you through grad school, and spent a fortune on you. And this is how you say thanks?*

Also taught me: It's true that the company has done a lot for me. It has also taught me to be ambitious. And you taught me to take advantage of my opportunities. I'd like your help.

Gets annoyed: *This isn't the way that you were looking for another job. I would've liked it if you told me earlier.*

No choice: I realize that and I'll do whatever I can to help. This was a completely unexpected solicitation—they came to me—but it is a once-in-a-lifetime opportunity. A positive recommendation from you would mean a great deal to me.

Still angry: *I don't know if you deserve it after what you're doing to me and the company.*

Reconsider: I don't think I'm doing anything you wouldn't do, if the situations were reversed. If you're saying you won't give me a positive reference, I'll just explain your reaction to my future employers. But I really hope you'll reconsider.

Accepting: *Listen, I'm not happy about your leaving, but I won't do anything to hurt your chances for this new job.*

Express thanks: Thank you, not just for your help in this, but throughout my time here. You've taught me a great deal and I'll always be grateful.

Still annoyed: *You know, the way you're handling this doesn't reflect well on you.*

No choice: I'm sorry you feel that way, but as I told you, I didn't seek this out. I know you wouldn't do anything to sidetrack my career. You've always helped me in the past, and I hope you will now.

ADAPTATIONS

This script can be modified to:

- Use a manager as a personal reference for a club, co-op, or part-time job.
- Use a manager's contacts for networking.
- Ask a supervisor to help you gain a promotion within the company.

KEY POINTS

- Present it as wonderful news you want to share.
- If he gets annoyed, stress the suddenness and uniqueness of your opportunity, as well as your willingness to do all you can to help concerning your replacement.
- If he says you're making a mistake, show him how the new job offers something this position cannot.
- If he explodes, counter his attacks and then show how the new job offers something your present position cannot.
- If he remains angry, reiterate the suddenness and uniqueness of your opportunity, frame his attitude as damaging to your future, and stress your willingness to do without his help.

Negotiating Severance with Your Former Boss

22.

STRATEGY

Severance packages are more negotiable than you may think. Treat them as preliminary offers, not done deals, and use whatever leverage you have. Even when standard packages are offered to a large group, exceptions can be made for special cases like yours. Do not sign a release—or even a statement acknowledging that you've been terminated—at the initial meeting when you receive the news. Insist on postponing all decisions to a subsequent meeting with both your immediate supervisor and someone from personnel. Say you need the time to digest the news or even that you feel too emotional to continue. Most reasonable employers will agree. If yours doesn't, simply say you're not feeling well, and you'll be back to finish the discussion first thing tomorrow, Then stand up and leave. What can she do? She has already fired you. Use the time before your subsequent meeting to determine your needs in terms of money and other benefits. Draft a memo outlining your dream severance package, listing a reason for each request. If you're a member of a protected minority, contact an employment lawyer. Put aside hurt and anger at your second meeting and instead, treat it like a business negotiation. Be firm in your demand for more, but flexible in what that constitutes. Know your bottom line. Keep in mind that both you and she want this wrapped up as soon as possible. If she tries to stonewall you, ask for another adjournment to speak with an attorney. The threat may break her resolve. If not, come back with another proposal the next day, either directly or through an attorney, if you have legal leverage.

TACTICS

- **Attitude:** Don't be fearful; you have nothing to lose. Be willing to use personal and legal leverage.
- **Preparation:** Analyze your needs and draft a memo outlining them. Speak with a lawyer, if you are a member of a protected minority.
- **Timing:** Do not sign anything until you've agreed on a package, and don't do that until a second meeting takes place.
- **Behavior:** Try to get beyond your anger and be as businesslike as possible. Roll up your sleeves and get down to serious horse trading—you want the deal done at this meeting.

22. Negotiating Severance with Your Former Boss

Deflect closing: I'm afraid I'm in no condition right now to sign anything or make any decisions. I need some time. I'd like to continue this discussion tomorrow afternoon instead.

The next day

Icebreaker and pitch: First, I'd like to thank you for agreeing to meet with me today. I've had a chance to go over your offer and I'd like to present my own proposal in response. I've seen that there's nothing out there in the job market, and it will take at least a year for me to find another position. Severance is supposed to bridge the gap between jobs, and what you're offering falls far short. I've taken the liberty of drafting a brief memo outlining my requests and the reasons for them. For example, I'd like one month's pay for each year I've been with the company. I'd like the company to continue to pay for my health insurance until I'm covered by a new employer. I'd like use of my office for another two weeks. And I'd like the company to provide at least four outplacement counseling sessions.

Against policy: *I'm sorry, but the package you were offered the other day is our only offer. Our policy is not to negotiate severance packages.*

Open to negotiation: *I'm willing to discuss your severance package, but I can't possibly provide all the things you've asked for in this memo.*

Wouldn't be fair: *I'm sorry, but the package you were offered the other day is our only offer. Negotiation with you wouldn't be fair to the others who were laid off.*

Special circumstances: I understand your need to be fair to all those who have been laid off, but I believe there are special circumstances in my case. Even though I have only been here for six months, I was recruited to come here from a job which I held for more than ten years.

Willing to compromise: I understand the constraints you're under. Why don't we just go over the items in my memo line by line. I'm not inflexible. I'm sure we can reach an agreement.

Exception to the rule: I understand your need to follow policy, but I believe my case is exceptional. I was recruited by you from another company and came here with the understanding I wouldn't lose the seniority I had at my prior job.

Imply legal action: I'm sorry as well. If that's the case, I must ask to adjourn this meeting in order to consult with my attorney. Either she or I will be back in touch with you shortly. Good day.

Still unwilling to negotiate: *I'm sorry. Whatever the facts of your case are, I simply cannot negotiate the severance package. That's our only [best] offer.*

KEY POINTS

- Put your anger aside and get down to business.
- If she cites policy, say you're an exception to the rule.
- If she cites the need for fairness, say yours is a special case.
- If she's open to negotiation, be ready to compromise.
- If she stonewalls, ask for another adjournment to speak with your lawyer or formulate another package.

II

...for Your Peers

Asking a Peer to Stop Back Stabbing

23

STRATEGY

The secret to stopping a back-stabbing peer is to show that the attacker, far from being constructive, is being unfair and personal. If the actions have been covert, deliver your message indirectly—that way the attacker can't simply deny involvement and end the conversation. If the attack was overt, or if the indirect approach doesn't work, deal directly. Ideally, you should conduct the discussion privately, which increases the chance of an honest exchange. But if that doesn't work, or if the attack is so damaging you must respond immediatcly, do it publicly. If all else fails, stress your willingness to take the dispute to a higher authority.

TACTICS

- **Attitude:** Don't feel defensive or uneasy. You are an aggrieved party looking for justice. You're coming from a position of honesty so you've a right to feel confident.
- **Preparation:** Jot down some notes about past attacks. For this script, they'll simply serve as reminders. If need be, they'll help you prepare a memo if this dialogue doesn't work.
- **Timing:** If the incident demands an immediate public response, do so. If not, approach the attacker privately as soon as possible after the latest attack.
- **Behavior:** Hold this meeting in the attacker's office. Don't schedule it—simply arrive. If this is an indirect approach, you can sit down. If this is a direct approach, shut the door behind you and remain standing, keeping yourself between him and the door. In effect, this puts you in the dominant position, keeps him a captive in his office, and forces him to listen to you. As soon as you finish your script, turn your back on him and leave.

23. Asking a Peer to Stop Back Stabbing

Indirect private approach

Icebreaker: I've heard that someone has been complaining that I'm not pulling my weight around here. What do you think I should do?

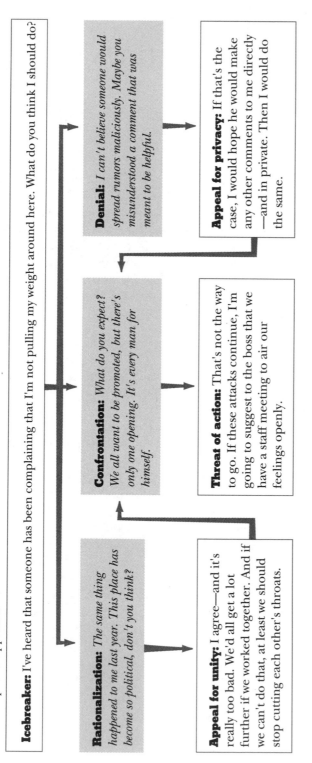

Denial: I can't believe someone would spread rumors maliciously. Maybe you misunderstood a comment that was meant to be helpful.

Appeal for privacy: If that's the case, I would hope he would make any other comments to me directly—and in private. Then I would do the same.

Confrontation: What do you expect? We all want to be promoted, but there's only one opening. It's every man for himself.

Threat of action: That's not the way to go. If these attacks continue, I'm going to suggest to the boss that we have a staff meeting to air our feelings openly.

Rationalization: The same thing happened to me last year. This place has become so political, don't you think?

Appeal for unity: I agree—and it's really too bad. We'd all get a lot further if we worked together. And if we can't do that, at least we should stop cutting each other's throats.

Direct public response/Private approach

Direct public response: I can't understand why you'd want to slander me this way in public. I suggest you stop this public display and discuss any personal problems we may have in private. But right now, I suggest we get back to business.

Later that day

Icebreaker: What have I ever done to you to elicit this kind of behavior? I can't imagine why you're attacking me.

Rationalization: *Last year, someone told the boss my staff was demoralized. I know it was you. I'm just responding in kind.*

Appeal for unity: I've never attacked you—that's not my style. I like working with you, not against you. But if we can't work together, I'd at least appreciate your cutting out the attacks.

Confrontation: *Listen, we all want this promotion. If you can't take the competition, maybe you ought to remove yourself.*

Threat of action: Listen, I'm for a fair fight. I know what you're doing. If you keep it up, I'll suggest we sit down with the boss and discuss our problems.

Denial: *I didn't attack you. I just pointed out a couple of mistakes you've made lately in the hope they won't happen again.*

Appeal for privacy: If you're really interested in helping me, come to me privately; don't bring things up at staff meetings. I'll do the same for you.

ADAPTATIONS

This script can be modified to:
- Confront a back-stabbing acquaintance or friend.
- Dispel a rumor.
- Handle an off-color joke.

KEY POINTS

- Respond in kind: indirectly to covert attacks, directly to overt attacks.
- If need be, respond publicly and immediately. Otherwise, have the discussion in private.
- If the attacker denies either being the perpetrator or that the attack was harmful, appeal for privacy.
- If the attacker rationalizes his action, appeal for unity.
- If the attacker is confrontational, threaten to bring the matter up with higher authorities or go public with it.

Tactfully Suggesting Better Hygiene to a Peer

24.

STRATEGY

Having to tell someone that her breath or body odor is offensive may be one of the most awkward situations you'll ever face in the workplace. Yet sometimes it's essential to take action, not only for the comfort of you and other coworkers, but for the company and the person's future as well. Such problems are almost certain to undermine the image of the company if the offender comes into contact with clients. Hygiene problems will erode her standing in the company and will block any further progress in the organization. Begin with the assumption that she isn't conscious of the problem. Start off by subtly suggesting the same tools you use to avoid similar problems. If she takes the hint, let the matter drop. If your subtext isn't understood, you'll have to press further while still being somewhat diplomatic.

TACTICS

- **Attitude:** Try not to be embarrassed. The other party will be embarrassed enough for both of you. Remember, you're doing this for her own good.
- **Preparation:** Buy some breath mints or look around for a nearby drugstore.
- **Timing:** Do this immediately after lunch and privately. That way you minimize embarrassment and have an excuse for your actions.
- **Behavior:** Start off subtly, but if necessary, shift to sincere concern. There's no need to be apologetic, because you're doing the person a favor.

24. Tactfully Suggesting Better Hygiene to a Peer

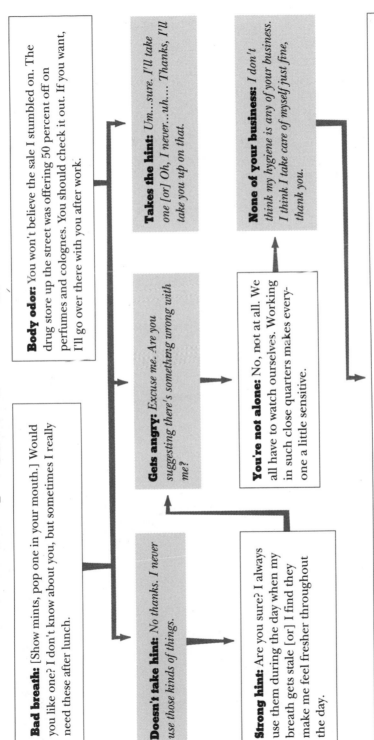

Bad breath: [Show mints, pop one in your mouth.] Would you like one? I don't know about you, but sometimes I really need these after lunch.

Body odor: You won't believe the sale I stumbled on. The drug store up the street was offering 50 percent off on perfumes and colognes. You should check it out. If you want, I'll go over there with you after work.

Doesn't take hint: *No thanks. I never use those kinds of things.*

Takes the hint: *Um…sure. I'll take one [or] Oh, I never…uh…. Thanks, I'll take you up on that.*

Gets angry: *Excuse me. Are you suggesting there's something wrong with me?*

Strong hint: Are you sure? I always use them during the day when my breath gets stale [or] I find they make me feel fresher throughout the day.

You're not alone: No, not at all. We all have to watch ourselves. Working in such close quarters makes everyone a little sensitive.

None of your business: *I don't think my hygiene is any of your business. I think I take care of myself just fine, thank you.*

We're in this together: Under most circumstances I'd agree with you. But we work in very close quarters here. I'd expect you to do the same thing for me if the situation were reversed. We have to take care of each other.

ADAPTATIONS

This script can be modified to:
- Discuss hygiene problems with a spouse.
- Discuss hygiene problems or erratic behavior with a parent or older relative.

KEY POINTS

- Start off subtly, but if necessary, be direct.
- If she takes the hint, drop the issue.
- If she doesn't take the hint, make your case stronger.
- If she gets angry, say it's a problem everyone there shares.
- If she says it's none of your business, explain why it is something you need to be concerned with.

Suggesting No Further Drinking to a Peer

25

STRATEGY

It's always awkward to discuss drinking habits with a colleague, but never more so than at a sales conference or in some other out-of-the-office business/personal situation. Most large companies have established routines for identifying, warning, and assisting employees who show signs of chronic alcohol or drug abuse. But when a fellow sales rep blows a deal by getting drunk at a client dinner, there's no employee-assistance program around to intervene. There's probably little you can do at the time, short of making a scene—and he has probably already taken care of that. So your goal is to make sure it doesn't happen again. That means changing his behavior—at least in his business meetings with you.

TACTICS

- **Attitude:** Be direct, clear, and determined. You are doing this for his good, your good, and the company's good, so there's no reason for you to question your actions.
- **Preparation:** Expect efforts either to deny there's a problem or to shift the focus of the discussion from the issue of drinking. Consider "compromise solutions" short of abstinence.
- **Timing:** Do this as soon as possible after an incident when the problem was obvious. Breakfast the morning after a botched client dinner is fine—as long as he isn't too hung over.
- **Behavior:** Be compassionate, but keep the focus on business. Your goal is to keep from being embarrassed in the future and to make sure his problem doesn't hurt your career.

25. Suggesting No Further Drinking to a Peer

Icebreaker: I need to speak with you about something that's affecting the way we work together. I think you need to stop drinking when we're working together. It's hurting our chances to close deals. Drinking gives clients an excuse to drink more and lets them avoid making decisions. And to be honest, sometimes you're not careful about what you're saying.

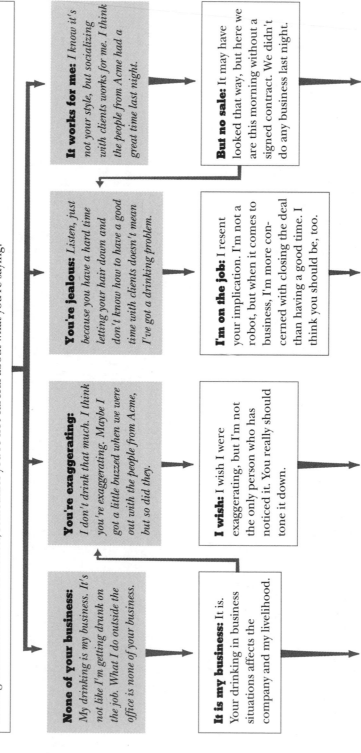

None of your business: *My drinking is my business. It's not like I'm getting drunk on the job. What I do outside the office is none of your business.*

It is my business: It is. Your drinking in business situations affects the company and my livelihood.

You're exaggerating: *I don't drink that much. I think you're exaggerating. Maybe I got a little buzzed when we were out with the people from Acme, but so did they.*

I wish: I wish I were exaggerating, but I'm not the only person who has noticed it. You really should tone it down.

You're jealous: *Listen, just because you have a hard time letting your hair down and don't know how to have a good time with clients doesn't mean I've got a drinking problem.*

I'm on the job: I resent your implication. I'm not a robot, but when it comes to business, I'm more concerned with closing the deal than having a good time. I think you should be, too.

It works for me: *I know it's not your style, but socializing with clients works for me. I think the people from Acme had a great time last night.*

But no sale: It may have looked that way, but here we are this morning without a signed contract. We didn't do any business last night.

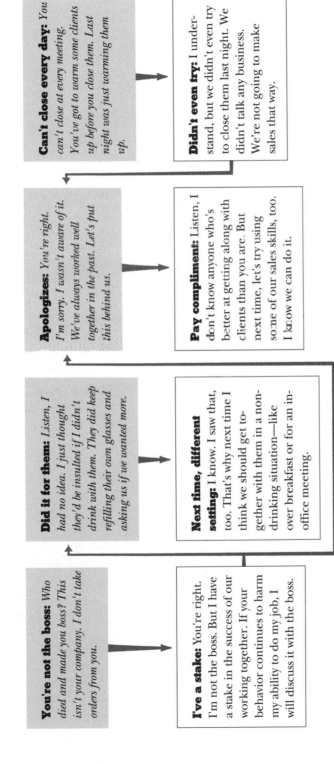

Can't close every day: *You can't close at every meeting. You've got to warm some clients up before you close them. Last night was just warming them up.*

Didn't even try: I understand, but we didn't even try to close them last night. We didn't talk any business. We're not going to make sales that way.

Apologizes: *You're right. I'm sorry. I wasn't aware of it. We've always worked well together in the past. Let's put this behind us.*

Pay compliment: Listen, I don't know anyone who's better at getting along with clients than you are. But next time, let's try using some of our sales skills, too. I know we can do it.

Did it for them: *Listen, I had no idea. I just thought they'd be insulted if I didn't drink with them. They did keep refilling their own glasses and asking us if we wanted more.*

Next time, different setting: I know. I saw that, too. That's why next time I think we should get together with them in a non-drinking situation—like over breakfast or for an in-office meeting.

You're not the boss: *Who died and made you boss? This isn't your company. I don't take orders from you.*

I've a stake: You're right. I'm not the boss. But I have a stake in the success of our working together. If your behavior continues to harm my ability to do my job, I will discuss it with the boss.

ADAPTATIONS

This script can be modified to:

- Address any form of antisocial behavior by a business peer.
- Discuss the physical appearance of a business peer.

KEY POINTS

- Be businesslike, determined, clear, and direct.
- If he says his drinking is none of your business, stress that when it happens in a work situation, it is your business.
- If he says you're exaggerating, say other people have noticed too.
- If he says you're too uptight, say you're simply interested in getting your job done.
- If he blames the clients, suggest having meetings at nondrinking times or places.
- If he accuses you of acting superior, just reiterate your stake in the situation.

Asking a Peer to Come in Earlier and/or Stay Later

26

STRATEGY

We've all been down *this* road: Saddled with extra work at the last minute, you and everyone else in your department start coming in early and/or staying late to complete it by a deadline—everyone else except one lone soul, that is. She's at her desk at nine and out the door exactly at five, and you're all getting pretty ticked. If she put in some extra time like the rest of you, everyone's burden would be eased. The goal of this script is to get Ms. Nine-to-Five to pull her weight and put in those extra hours like everyone else. Your first strategy will be to appeal to her sense of fairness. Point out the rewards of coming in early and/or staying late, whether it's the bonus the department has been promised or simply getting the work done faster. Remind her she won't have to put in these hours forever. If these tactics fail, point out that she's rapidly becoming an object of hatred among her peers. Unfortunately, some people don't care if coworkers dislike them. If even the threat of becoming a pariah fails, it's time to use your final weapon: Let her know that if there's a problem with the project and the boss is looking for scapegoats, her name is likely to be number one on everyone's list.

TACTICS

- **Attitude:** Your attitude should be one of asking for help without resorting to begging, cajoling, or threatening. It's OK if she gets an inkling of how angry you and the rest of the department are, as long as your dissatisfaction with her isn't conveyed blatantly via yelling, cursing, or name-calling.
- **Preparation:** Talk with others in your department and let them know you plan on approaching her—alone—about her unwillingness to put in extra time. Tell those who disagree that while they may feel differently about the situation than you, you'd appreciate it if they didn't tip your hand. Ask those who agree if they'd be willing to back you up if she demands proof that others feel as you do. If applicable, be able to provide concrete examples for her of how her refusal to come in early and/or stay late has hurt the department.

26. Asking a Peer to Come in Earlier and/or Stay Later

Appeal to sense of fairness: Hey, Paula, got a minute? You know that project the sales department dumped on us at the last minute? Well, the rest of us have been either coming in early or staying late trying to get it done on time, and we could really use your help. Would you mind putting in a little extra time?

Doesn't want to know: *I hear you, but can I point something out? I don't see the sales department burning the midnight oil or showing up at the crack of dawn. We didn't create this problem; why should we have to pick up the slack?*

Grow up: Because picking up the slack is our job, Paula. Look, haven't there been times in the past when we've done the same thing to sales? It's just the nature of the beast. Besides, if we get this done on time we'll be up for a bonus, and we'll be able to kick back for awhile.

Scheduling problem: *I don't know if I can. I usually shoot right over to day-care after work to pick up Jamie, and if I come in early, it's going to mess up the whole family's schedule, since I'm the one who gets Ruthie off to school so Sam can get to his office early.*

Sympathy for scheduling, but...: Geez, Paula, I didn't realize you and Sam were juggling so many balls outside work. But, you know, so are a couple of other people, and they've been able to make temporary arrangements just until the project is completed. Maybe you could ask them what they did. We're not going to be swamped like this forever.

Refuses: *No way. They're not paying us overtime! Besides, I already give enough of my life to this stinkin' company!*

Rationality and guilt: We're not being paid by the hour, Paula, we're being paid a salary. And while I might identify with not wanting to give the company a minute more than you must, the truth is, it's your coworkers you're screwing. And people are starting to get annoyed.

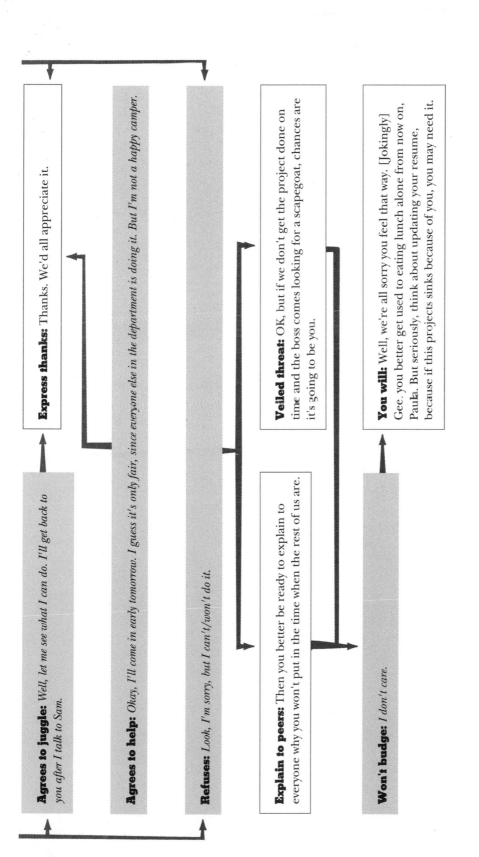

Agrees to juggle: *Well, let me see what I can do. I'll get back to you after I talk to Sam.*

Agrees to help: *Okay, I'll come in early tomorrow. I guess it's only fair, since everyone else in the department is doing it. But I'm not a happy camper.*

Refuses: *Look, I'm sorry, but I can't/won't do it.*

Explain to peers: Then you better be ready to explain to everyone why you won't put in the time when the rest of us are.

Won't budge: *I don't care.*

Express thanks: Thanks. We'd all appreciate it.

Veiled threat: OK, but if we don't get the project done on time and the boss comes looking for a scapegoat, chances are it's going to be you.

You will: Well, we're all sorry you feel that way. [Jokingly] Gee, you better get used to eating lunch alone from now on, Paula. But seriously, think about updating your resume, because if this projects sinks because of you, you may need it.

- **Timing:** Talk to her while the project is still in progress, not after it's completed. Make sure the two of you are alone. After lunch is always a good time to talk to a peer, since satiated people tend to be in a decent mood. Avoid approaching her when she's on her way out the door at the end of the day; what you say will go in one ear and out the other.
- **Behavior:** Start out politely, appealing to her sense of fairness. If she refuses to even consider what you're saying, it's OK to throw a touch of annoyance into the mix. Don't be afraid of using a veiled threat, either. Whatever you do, don't beg or yell.

ADAPTATIONS

This script can be modified to:

- Request a friend, relative, or spouse to pull their weight on a joint project, whether it's planning a party or keeping a house clean.

KEY POINTS

- Get the backing of your coworkers before talking to her.
- Talk to her while the project is still under way.
- If applicable, be able to provide concrete examples of how her unwillingness to put in extra time has adversely affected the department.
- Appeal to her sense of fairness, pointing out she's the only person in the department who isn't coming in early or staying late.
- If that fails, make her feel guilty for not pulling her weight like everyone else.
- Point out the benefits of coming in early and/or staying late, such as the potential for a bonus, easing the work burden for everyone, and getting the project done that much faster.
- Point out the drawbacks of her behavior, such as alienating her coworkers.
- If you must, threaten her with telling the boss she's to blame should the project not be finished on time.
- Don't beg, cajole, or threaten.
- Let a touch of anger show if necessary, but don't yell or belittle.

Asking a Peer to Improve the Quality of His Work

27

STRATEGY

Most of us get along swimmingly with our coworkers, which is why it can be so disconcerting when the quality of a peer's work begins to slide. Where once the two of you functioned like a well-oiled machine, you now find that your job is harder to do either because (a) you're trying to compensate for his sloppiness, laziness, or inattentiveness or (b) the caliber of *your* work is slipping because it's contingent on the quality of his. The goal of this lifescript is getting a peer to improve the quality of his work without harming your professional relationship and/or coming across as holier-than-thou. Your first gambit will be to appeal to his sense of fairness, pointing out it isn't right you should suffer because he's turning out subpar work. That means you'll need to be able to prove his work "isn't what it used to be," as well as show how it's affecting you. If, after receiving concrete evidence of his lackluster performance, he *still* insists he's the best worker bee on the planet, resort to your most powerful gambit: making the boss aware that the inferior quality of his work is having a deleterious effect on yours.

TACTICS

- **Attitude:** Even if you're ready to blow a gasket, your attitude should be one of asking for help. Never resort to begging, yelling, or threats. If you can't kill him with kindness, you could turn the heat up a notch and show how ticked off you are—again, without blowing up. Just be aware that in showing any annoyance, you could alienate him. Cool, calm, and collected always work best.
- **Preparation:** Before you confront him and tell him in the nicest way possible that his work leaves a lot to be desired, you need evidence that demonstrates not only that this is true, but also that the inferior quality of his work is making it hard for you to maintain your own high standards. Any concrete examples you can point to will be useful, but written work showing when he hits his marks and when he doesn't is the most powerful.
- **Timing:** If you can, try talking to him before the two of you embark on another project together, or while you're in the midst of one. Speak with him alone, preferably not first thing in the morning or when he's dashing out the door at the end of the day. Behind closed doors right after lunch is ideal.

109

27. Asking a Peer to Improve the Quality of His Work

Icebreaker: Walt, have you got a minute? I need to talk to you. You know I really enjoy working with you. But lately, the research you've been giving me has had some major holes in it, and it's really made it hard for me to turn in reports up to the boss's standards. I was wondering, could you possibly kick up the level of your work a bit?

Denial: *What are you talking about? My work is fine.*

Confront denial: I'm talking about the fact that the info you gave me for the Johnson report was two years out of date. If I didn't depend on you, it wouldn't matter to me. But I do depend on you, and it kind of bothers me that my work now looks bad because you're cutting corners. It's not fair.

Still defensive: *Are you threatening me?*

Anger: *No offense, but who died and made you boss? My work is fine.*

Deflect anger: I'm not trying to be the boss, and God knows I never claimed to be perfect. All I'm asking is that you give one hundred percent like you always did in the past, so I'm not stuck doing double time to make things right. Think how you'd feel if you were in my shoes.

Admits guilt: *I know, I know, you're right. What do you need me to do?*

Admission of guilt: *I'm sorry, Phil, but I've got a lot on my mind right now. I'm doing the best I can.*

Accept apology: I hear you. I know how hard it can be to keep your mind on work when there are a lot of outside distractions. But it would really mean a lot to me if you'd try. Besides, throwing yourself into work might even make you feel better.

Agrees to try: *Hmmm, maybe you're right. I'll give it a try.*

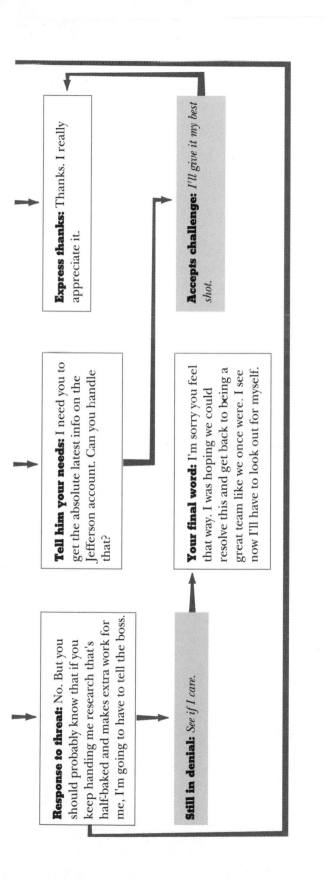

Response to threat: No. But you should probably know that if you keep handing me research that's half-baked and makes extra work for me, I'm going to have to tell the boss.

Tell him your needs: I need you to get the absolute latest info on the Jefferson account. Can you handle that?

Express thanks: Thanks. I really appreciate it.

Still in denial: *See if I care.*

Your final word: I'm sorry you feel that way. I was hoping we could resolve this and get back to being a great team like we once were. I see now I'll have to look out for myself.

Accepts challenge: *I'll give it my best shot.*

- **Behavior:** You might be feeling virtuous because your work isn't inferior—at least, it wasn't until *he* started fouling you up—but whatever you do, don't come across that way. Act as if he's a valued colleague whose help you need. If push comes to shove, make it clear—politely, of course—that you're not going to let him drag you down with him.

ADAPTATIONS

This script can be modified to:
- Ask a child to improve the quality of his housework.
- Ask a spouse to improve the quality of his housework.
- Ask a partner to improve the quality of his work.

KEY POINTS

- Appeal to his sense of fairness, making it clear that his sloppy and/or subpar work is having a direct effect on your work.
- Be able to provide concrete evidence of above.
- If asking him to improve fails, threaten to tell a superior what's going on.
- Don't beg, yell, or belittle.
- Don't lose your temper.
- Approach him as a valued colleague to whom you're appealing for help.
- Speak with him alone, preferably after lunch.
- Be calm and polite no matter how abusive, upset, or defensive he might become.

Asking a Peer to Stop Gossiping

28.

STRATEGY

When you're the subject of gossip, your natural instinct might be to lash out at the person you suspect is playing Gossip Columnist and give her a piece of your mind. Don't. The goal of this script is to help you convey your displeasure with her tongue wagging—and to get her to stop—without a direct accusation. This is important, since *(a)* you could be accusing her falsely; *(b)* confrontation could disrupt your work relationship; or *(c)* you could cause the other person, if spiteful, to spread even more falsehoods designed to damage your reputation, both personal and professional. For this lifescript to work, you can't let on you know you're talking to a gossip. Instead, approach the gossiper as if you're confiding in her about what has taken place.

TACTICS

- **Attitude:** Depending on what has been said, you might be furious, wounded, or worried. Don't let it show. Instead, act calm. Your attitude should be one of disbelief at the gossiper's unprofessional behavior, tempered with annoyance at being the subject of office chatter.
- **Preparation:** Gossip spreads geometrically; while it usually springs from one source, before long lots of folks are telling the same tale. For that reason, it's crucial you be as sure as you can you're dealing with the original perpetrator. Ask around. Eventually, you'll be able to deduce who the motormouth is.
- **Timing:** Enticing as it might be to imagine your talk taking place in full view of the whole company in the employee cafeteria, this discussion should take place in private. If you must, come in early to catch her alone or ask her to stay after work for a few minutes. If either of you have your own office, do it there, preferably after lunch, when people are usually in a good mood. An empty rest room can work, too, although you risk interruption. If you must, talk to her quietly in the hall.
- **Behavior:** Remaining calm throughout, approach her as if you're troubled and seeking her advice. Segue into disbelief followed by mild indignation. Finally, ask her to help you squash the gossip. Don't say or do anything that tips your hand and makes it obvious you know it's she, whether by smirking, glaring, or being sarcastic.

28. Asking a Peer to Stop Gossiping

Icebreaker: Sarah, can I talk to you? I'm so upset. Someone is going around telling everyone I'm dating Drew. Can you believe that?

Defensive: *Who told you that?*

Response to defensiveness: What does that matter?

Confronts you: *But it's true, isn't it?*

Response to confrontation: That's not the point. It's nobody's business.

Backs off: *I was just curious.*

Ask for help: If you know who's spreading this story, it would really mean a lot to me if you could tell them to stop. It's really upsetting me.

Plays dumb: *That's awful! Do you know who?*

Response to ignorance: No, but I wish they'd stop. It's bound to make them, as well as me, look unprofessional.

Attempt to diffuse anger: *C'mon, lighten up. You know what it's like around here. Everyone talks about everyone else.*

Rebuff diffusing: It's one thing if it had to do with work. But this is my personal life.

Assuaging guilt: *I'm sure whoever has been talking didn't mean it maliciously.*

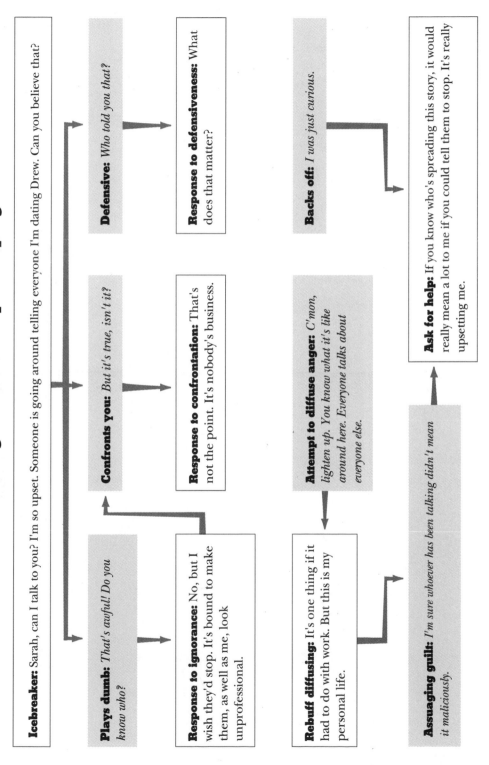

ADAPTATIONS

This script can be modified to:
- Nip gossiping by a friend or family member in the bud.
- Derail gossiping about a friend or coworker.

KEY POINTS

- Avoid direct confrontation.
- Make sure you've got the right person.
- Pretend you're confiding about how upset you are.
- Express your anger and disgust at the gossiper's unprofessional behavior.
- Finish by asking for her help in curbing the gossip, reiterating your distress.
- Keep calm, never letting on you're fully aware she is the guilty party.
- Don't smirk, glare, or use sarcasm.
- Have the discussion in private, if possible.

Correcting a Peer's Mistakes

29.

STRATEGY

In the workplace, handling the mistakes of a fellow worker requires a delicate touch. You need to deliver your message strongly enough so your help is heard and understood, but subtly enough so it doesn't undermine operations or create resentment. The secret is to present yourself as a friend, someone who has been through the situation before and can help. Outline the nature of the mistake and why it causes others problems, but affirm your confidence in your peer's abilities. If your comments are received favorably, suggest ways to correct the mistakes, then offer to be available for questions and help. If your peer disagrees with your perception or gets angry, remain calm, but restate your prior comments and how the mistakes interfere with efficiency. He must be made to understand that either he corrects his mistakes or you'll go over his head.

TACTICS

- **Attitude:** Think of yourself as a friend, even a mentor, someone who has been where this person is and can help. Be prepared to accept a little anger or frustration—criticism is never an easy pill to swallow, especially when given by a peer.
- **Preparation:** Have examples in mind so you can stay on the topic and give detailed and accurate information. Also, have specific suggestions ready to offer.
- **Timing:** Meet as soon as possible after the offense occurs so it's fresh in both your minds. Do it when you're alone, but don't make it seem like an ambush.
- **Behavior:** Remember, you're both in the same boat, so you want to help, not hurt. Lead off empathetically. If that doesn't work, make it clear you need to maintain a good, positive working relationship, so correcting each other's mistakes is essential.

29. Correcting a Peer's Mistakes

Icebreaker: Jeez, isn't the filing system confusing? It has taken me ages to get it straight. It totally defies logic—you'd think accounts would be filed under clients' names, but they're kept under product. Maybe that's why some of your account files have been popping up in weird places. I lost half a day searching for one of them.

Accepts criticism: *You had trouble with it, too? That's good to know. I'm trying really hard to get the hang of it. I didn't realize I was causing so much confusion. I'll have to think twice before I file!*

Denies the problem: *What are you talking about? No one else said anything to me. I'm pretty careful about where I put my files. Maybe you should check with everyone in the department—could be someone else is confused.*

Gets angry: *My files? No way! Who are you to get on my back about filing problems? I know what I am doing. You do your work, and I'll do mine. Anyway, nobody's perfect.*

Reiterate your point: Don't you handle the Joyce and O'Casey accounts? You wouldn't believe where I found them, and it's not the first time. You know what I do? I think about their product as I go for their file.

Defuse the anger: Hey, relax. I told you, I only figured out the system a short time ago myself. Someone mentioned it to me at the time, and I realized my mistakes were slowing the whole office down. I'm not trying to come down on you, just letting you know we all have to be really careful.

Gets past denial: *Yeah, they're mine. Did I put them in the wrong place again? I'm kind of glad you brought this up—I've been embarrassed I was having so much trouble with the system. I'll try to be more careful next time.*

Still denies the problem: *Sure, those are my account files, but I'm not the only who ever pulls them. Someone else in the department might have moved them, not me.*

Remains angry: *I really can't believe you're pulling rank on me. You really think you run this department, don't you? Well, I already have one boss, and that's quite enough. Worry about your own performance, not mine.*

Gets past the anger: *I'm sorry I snapped. I'm on deadline for this proposal, and the pressure is really on. Thanks for the warning.*

Get tough: OK. I just tried to help. You need to realize that when you misplace files, it throws everyone else off. I'd hate to do it, but if things don't get better, I'll have to speak to Vincent and see if he can help.

Offer to help: Don't sweat it. If you have any questions, feel free to ask me. Like I said, it can get pretty confusing, and we all have enough to do without worrying about filing, too.

ADAPTATIONS

This script can be modified to:

- Correct a friend, acquaintance, or fellow volunteer whose mistakes are effecting your efforts.

KEY POINTS

- Soften initial criticism by being empathetic, sharing your understanding of the problem.
- If your criticism isn't accepted, show your evidence without becoming defensive or angry yourself. Reaffirm your empathy and understanding, but remain firm.
- If your criticism meets with anger, remain calm, then reassure that you're only trying to help.
- If he accepts your criticism, reassert your desire to help anytime.
- If anger and/or denial continue, make it clear you were trying to help, but that resistance could call for further action, since mistakes affect productivity.
- Remember the goal is a successful, productive, stress-free work environment. You don't want to alienate or polarize, but you do want to be able to get your work done efficiently.

Refusing to Lie for a Peer

30

STRATEGY

When a peer asks you to lie, chances are it's to avoid getting in hot water with the boss for something she did or didn't do. Since you don't want to get a reputation as a liar or appear to be a partner in crime—both of which could jeopardize *your* job—the goal of this script is to make clear to your peer that you won't lie without sounding as condescending or holier-than-thou. Basically, you're walking a tightrope between maintaining good relations with your coworker and your boss. If this is the first time the coworker has asked for your "help," you can lean a little to her side of the tightrope. If this is clearly a habitual problem, lean toward your boss's side. But if this incident falls somewhere between unique and habitual, you'll have to try to strike a balance.

TACTICS

- **Attitude:** Whether it's the first time or the fiftieth she's asking you to cover for her, stand firm. Don't lose your temper or belittle her for screwing up. If it's the first time she has come to you, tell her you'll exaggerate the reasons for her behavior when relating the story to the boss and leave it at that. If she appears to be falling into a pattern of bad behavior and subsequently asking you to lie, calmly point out she'd better make an effort to change her behavior. If she's clearly a habitual offender, despite your prior warnings to her, feel free to bluntly convey your annoyance, saying in no uncertain terms that lying is out of the question.
- **Preparation:** There's no way to prepare for this situation, other than realizing that if you're there when she loses it, chances are she's going to ask your help in covering her butt.
- **Timing:** You can't control the timing of her approach, but you can control the timing of your response. If she asks you to lie for her in front of customers, tell her you'll discuss it later. If she asks you in front of other coworkers, deal with it immediately. That will send a clear message to all present that you don't consider lying for peers part of your job description.
- **Behavior:** Even if your track record is spotless, avoid pointing this out, as you'll sound pompous and condescending. Instead, be firm but friendly, even if she becomes increasingly distressed by your unwillingness to "help."

121

30. Refusing to Lie for a Peer

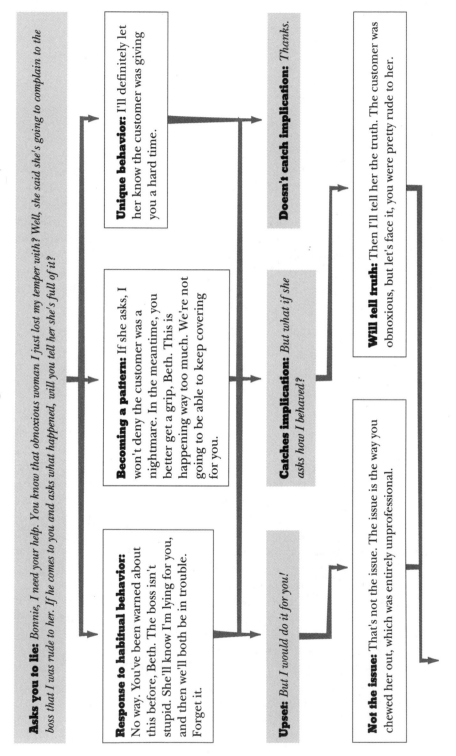

Asks you to lie: *Bonnie, I need your help. You know that obnoxious woman I just lost my temper with? Well, she said she's going to complain to the boss that I was rude to her. If he comes to you and asks what happened, will you tell her she's full of it?*

Unique behavior: I'll definitely let her know the customer was giving you a hard time.

Doesn't catch implication: *Thanks.*

Becoming a pattern: If she asks, I won't deny the customer was a nightmare. In the meantime, you better get a grip, Beth. This is happening way too much. We're not going to be able to keep covering for you.

Catches implication: *But what if she asks how I behaved?*

Will tell truth: Then I'll tell her the truth. The customer was obnoxious, but let's face it, you were pretty rude to her.

Response to habitual behavior: No way. You've been warned about this before, Beth. The boss isn't stupid. She'll know I'm lying for you, and then we'll both be in trouble. Forget it.

Upset: *But I would do it for you!*

Not the issue: That's not the issue. The issue is the way you chewed her out, which was entirely unprofessional.

Defends himself: *But you saw what she was like!*

That's no excuse: You're right. But you know the rule: The customer is always right.

Final appeal: *So you're not going to help me?*

Final advice: I'll help you, but I'm not going to lie for you. My advice is that you better get your act together when it comes to dealing with the customers. If you don't, you might lose your job.

ADAPTATIONS

This script can be modified to:

- Respond to a request to lie in any situation that may jeopardize a personal or business relationship.

KEY POINTS

- Be firm, but friendly, in your refusal to lie.
- Don't lose your temper or humiliate the other person.
- Avoid blowing your own horn.
- If it's the first time she asks, offer gentle corrections.
- If it has happened before, warn her this behavior could get her into trouble and advise her to change.
- If the behavior is habitual, tell her you refuse to compromise your credibility and risk your job for her.
- Respond to a request immediately if coworkers are present.
- Postpone the conversation if you're approached in front of clients or customers.

Telling a Peer to Stop Harassing You

31.

STRATEGY

Despite the trepidation and fear involved, if you're being harassed, you must deal with it immediately. If you don't put an end to the harassment, it will only escalate. The key to stopping harassment is to present a powerful, unequivocal objection, whatever the type of harassment and regardless of the harasser's motivations. An off-color joke should be treated with the same urgency as a pinch. Otherwise, your complaint won't be taken seriously. In many of these cases, power is as much an issue as sex. That's why you need to seize the power in this confrontation. You can do that by launching a direct assault.

TACTICS

- **Attitude:** All types of harassment are equal and require the same response—a powerful direct assault.
- **Preparation:** If you anticipate trouble, speak with a higher-up or the human resources department prior to the meeting.
- **Timing:** Deal with it as soon as possible. Delay will only empower the harasser and make you feel powerless.
- **Behavior:** Go to his office or workspace, position yourself between him and the door so he cannot leave, remain standing, maintain eye contact throughout, and walk out as soon as you're done, ensuring that you have the final word.

31. Telling a Peer to Stop Harassing You

Icebreaker: I want you to stop working and listen very carefully to what I'm about to say.

You're overreacting: *Relax, you're overreacting. It was just a joke. Don't take everything so seriously! Why don't you cool off a bit and we'll forget all about it, OK?*

Implied threat: Your behavior toward me is totally unacceptable and must stop right now.

Your word against mine: *Ooh, I love it when you get mad. But seriously, babe, it's just your word against mine. And no one is going to believe you. So why don't you forget all about this and let's go out to lunch.*

Refuse to play games: This is my profession. Ours is a business relationship, period. I come here to work, not to play games.

I'm sorry: *I'm sorry. I didn't mean anything by it. I was just joking. I didn't realize it would offend you. Can't we just forget all about it?*

Beat him to punch: I thought you might respond this way, so I made sure to speak with personnel before I came here. They told me to speak to you prior to filing a formal complaint.

You're too sensitive: *Hold your horses. I said I didn't mean anything by it. You're exaggerating the importance of this. I really think you're being too sensitive.*

Put him on notice: I hear your apology, but there's no excuse for that kind of behavior. I've prepared a memo outlining what happened, but I'll hold on to it for now. Maybe you'll be able to work things out.

You can't hurt me: *You don't scare me. I can make your life here miserable and destroy your future in this business. Go ahead. File your complaint. Nothing will happen to me.*

Imply legal action: That's not what my lawyer says.

ADAPTATIONS

This script can be modified to:
- Counter any type of on-the-job extortion.
- Counter an announced threat to your position by a coworker.

KEY POINTS

- Be as forceful as possible in your opening statement.
- Stress that there will be repercussions to continued harassment.
- If he says you're overreacting, state that this is a place of business, not a social club.
- If he says it's your word against his, explain that you've already gone to higher-ups.
- If he apologizes, say there's no excuse for his actions, but you'll hold off taking further action for now.
- If he says that you're too sensitive or that there's nothing you can do, say your lawyer disagrees.

Asking a Peer to Clean Up Her Work Area

32.

STRATEGY

You probably won't care if the gal in the next cubicle is the reincarnation of Oscar Madison until you have a hard time finding something you need in her workspace; her mess starts spreading into communal or your own workspace; or the boss starts referring to your whole department as "the pit." The goal of this script is to get your coworker to clean up her work area as soon as it affects either your reputation or your ability to do your job. Without calling her a slob—at least, not to her face—you need to make it clear that if she doesn't tidy up and provide easy access to material others need, you'll be forced to blow the whistle. Avoid making comparisons or offering put-downs. If she acknowledges her desk is a mess, offer to help. If she gets defensive, point out how the six-foot-high piles of files and faxes reflect badly on the whole department. If she insists that only she needs to know where everything is, calmly bring to her attention the information she keeps that you require as well, and subtly threaten a trip to the boss if she doesn't get her act together. If she says she can't stand the thought of your nosing through her things, tell her all she needs to do is separate work items from personal items, and the problem is solved.

TACTICS

- **Attitude:** Most people aren't deliberately messy. A few are, however. They believe making things difficult for others to find makes them indispensable. But even if you think this description fits your coworker, you can't call her on it without causing a major upset. Your attitude should always be one of offering friendly advice.
- **Preparation:** Your request needs to be backed up with a concrete example of how her sloppiness has negatively affected you, whether it was a disparaging comment made by management, or your being late to a meeting because you couldn't find the sales report that was supposed to be in her out basket.
- **Timing:** You need to speak with her as soon as possible after something has happened.
- **Behavior:** Don't confront her in front of anyone else in the office. If you do, embarrassment might compel her to make things really difficult for you to find. Don't yell, beg, or belittle. Though you might be tempted to touch things in her workspace to drive your point home, don't—if she's very jealous of her privacy, that could send her over the edge.

32. Asking a Peer to Clean Up Her Work Area

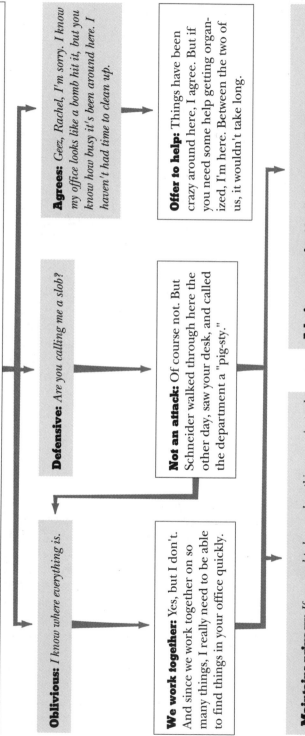

Icebreaker: Thelma, I need to speak with you. You know the report we've been working on? Well, Schneider asked to see it on Friday when you were out. It took me twenty minutes just to find it under all that stuff you have piled on your desk. I really think you need to clean up your work area.

Oblivious: *I know where everything is.*

Defensive: *Are you calling me a slob?*

We work together: Yes, but I don't. And since we work together on so many things, I really need to be able to find things in your office quickly.

Not an attack: Of course not. But Schneider walked through here the other day, saw your desk, and called the department a "pig-sty."

Agrees: *Geez, Rachel, I'm sorry. I know my office looks like a bomb hit it, but you know how busy it's been around here. I haven't had time to clean up.*

Offer to help: Things have been crazy around here, I agree. But if you need some help getting organized, I'm here. Between the two of us, it wouldn't take long.

Admits paranoia: *No offense, Rachel, but I hate the thought of anyone going through my things when I'm not here.*

Maintains privacy: *If you need to know where things are, just ask. You can even call me at home.*

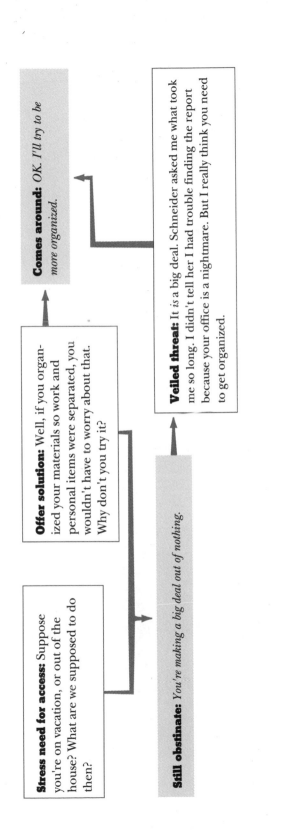

Stress need for access: Suppose you're on vacation, or out of the house? What are we supposed to do then?

Offer solution: Well, if you organized your materials so work and personal items were separated, you wouldn't have to worry about that. Why don't you try it?

Comes around: *OK. I'll try to be more organized.*

Still obstinate: *You're making a big deal out of nothing.*

Veiled threat: It *is* a big deal. Schneider asked me what took me so long. I didn't tell her I had trouble finding the report because your office is a nightmare. But I really think you need to get organized.

ADAPTATIONS

This script can be modified to:

- Help you convince a spouse, roommate, partner, friend, or family member to keep her room, house, or car neater.

KEY POINTS

- Act as if you're giving friendly advice.
- Avoid coming across as superior. Don't put her down.
- Don't touch her things.
- Have a concrete example of how the sloppiness has affected you.
- Speak with her as soon as possible after something has occurred.
- Speak with her in private.
- If she admits her work area is a mess, offer to help her clean it.
- If she challenges you, point out how her messiness makes everyone look bad.
- If she claims only she needs to know where things are, have an example of why that isn't true.
- If she says she doesn't like anyone going through her things, suggest she separate work items from personal items.
- If nothing else works, issue a veiled threat.

Confronting a
Pilfering Peer

33

STRATEGY

Floppy disks, toilet paper, rubber bands, file folders, legal pads—when it comes to items people steal from the workplace, the list is endless. The goal of this lifescript is to stop a pilfering peer without coming across as smug, saintly, or a member of the FBI. Caught red-handed and confronted in a *gentle* way (yelling "Up against the wall, sucka" is a bad move), your coworker will either fall to his knees and beg you not to tell the Suits; snarl that the very least the company owes him is a case of paper clips, since they pay coolie wages; or minimize his foray into larceny by claiming it's something everyone does. If he's got an iota of conscience and common sense, he'll see the error of his ways (after you point them out to him, of course) and put the goods back voluntarily. But if he doesn't, you need to make it clear that if you catch him stealing again, and you're later asked if you know who made off with the couch from the employees' lounge, you're not going to cover for him.

TACTICS

- **Attitude:** Whether you're shocked by your coworkers stealing from the office or secretly wish you had the guts to do it yourself, your attitude should be calm yet no-nonsense disapproval. Whatever you do, don't come across as morally superior, or you'll have an enemy for life.
- **Preparation:** Unfortunately, there's little you can do to prepare for this discussion, since it's likely to arise spontaneously the minute you come across your pilfering peer in action.
- **Timing:** Confront your peer the minute you catch him in the act—not after, or before he strikes again.
- **Behavior:** You're neither Sherlock Holmes nor the Pope, so avoid behaving like either. Be supremely cool and calm, making your first volley on the light side, if possible. Don't try to wrest the pilfered item from his sticky fingers; similarly, avoid standing there smugly with your arms crossed like a disapproving schoolmarm. On the other hand, maintain eye contact at all times.

33. Confronting a Pilfering Peer

Icebreaker: Tom? I can't help but notice that's a whole case of floppies you're putting in your briefcase. Taking one disk to bring home is one thing; but the big guys are definitely going to notice if a whole case is missing. You sure you want to do that?

Unashamed: *What's the big deal? Everyone does it.*

Rationalizing: *Why the heck should I pay for this when the company pays us slave wages? Besides, they consider this part of our "compensation." They owe me this.*

Frightened: *Oh my God, Dan, please don't tell the boss.*

Appeal to conscience: That's not true. I don't do it. And even if everyone did do it, that still doesn't make it the right or the smart thing to do.

Appeal to rationality: I hear you, and you're right: The pay around here leaves a lot to be desired. But if you're caught, your job could be in jeopardy. And if they find out I knew and covered for you, I could be in trouble, too. Besides, if stuff keeps disappearing, they'll keep using it as an excuse not to give us a raise. I think you should put it back.

Allay his fear: Mum's the word, if you put it back.

Sees the light: *You're right. I'll put it back.*

Now mad at you: *Hey, mind your own business, OK? Who do you think you are, anyway? Mother Theresa?*

Parting words: No, St. Francis. Seriously though, I'm not joking around. I'm not going to bust you this time. But if it happens again and the boss comes creeping around trying to find out who stole what, I'm not going to cover for you, either.

ADAPTATIONS

This script can be modified to:

- Confront a pilfering relative, friend, or guest.

KEY POINTS

- Keep your tone light.
- Confront him the minute you come upon him stealing.
- Avoid acting like a member of the CIA or the Vatican.
- Appeal to his conscience. If he doesn't have one, make it clear you won't cover for him if the suits come snooping around wanting to know who has sticky fingers.
- Maintain eye contact.

Asking a Peer to Cover for You

34.

STRATEGY

The goal of this script is getting a coworker to cover for you when you have personal business to take care of outside the office, but don't want to lose a personal/sick day. First a warning: If you're on probation or have been warned in any way about absenteeism, do not use this script—it's too dangerous. If you ask someone and get turned down, you won't be able to ask someone else without the risk of being discovered. Your only option will be to take time off without pay or use a sick day. The secret to achieving your goal is to encourage an immediate, albeit subtly subconscious, receptivity to your pitch on the part of the listener. You can do that by making her feel important—you're turning to her for help rather than to someone else. Opening with a heartfelt appeal helps, too—after all, no one likes to refuse a request for help. If you're sure she won't gossip, you can be as specific as you please in furnishing the details of your absence. If, on the other hand, you're afraid the word might spread, be as vague as possible, saying only that you have some personal business to attend to. If pressed for more information, say you prefer not to talk about it. Be aware, however, that a refusal to provide the gory details could lead to a flat-out refusal to help. Consider subtly pointing out how assistance can benefit her, whether it's a promise of reciprocity or a more manageable workload.

TACTICS

- **Attitude:** Your attitude should be one of humility, whether you're asking a good friend or an acquaintance. Opening with a statement like, "I need your help" establishes that tone.
- **Preparation:** Guesstimate how long you'll be out of the office before approaching your peer. In addition, try to discern her attitude toward using work time to attend to personal biz. Some people go strictly by the book and look down on those who bend the rules, whereas others are always glad to help out with any activity that "cheats the suits." Have a backup plan in mind, just in case you find out your first choice isn't apt to go along with you.
- **Timing:** Ask for help at least a few days in advance. That way you'll have time to implement your back-up plan, if necessary. After lunch is usually the best time for a private conversation like this.

34. Asking a Peer to Cover for You

Icebreaker and pitch: Melanie, I need your help. I have to take a few hours off Thursday afternoon. Normally, I would just call in sick, but we're so swamped and I don't want us to fall too far behind because I'm out for a whole day. If the boss asks where I am, could you tell her that I'm [mention a work-related errand] and will be back at [fill in the time].

Curious: *Where are you going?*

Scared: *No way. You know what a grump the boss has been lately. I can't cover for you and risk getting in trouble.*

Mercenary: *Depends. What's in it for me?*

Deflect curiosity: I have some personal business I need to take care of.

Assuage fear: I don't think it's much of a risk. Besides, it would benefit you.

Quid pro quo: First, you won't be doing all our work by yourself all day, which you would be if I have to call in sick. Second, you know I would do it for you, if you asked. And third, you'd be helping me out tremendously.

Pushes for details: *What kind of personal business?*

Refuses: *Sorry, no can do.*

Agrees: *Okay, I'll cover for you. But what exactly should I tell the boss if she asks?*

Remain vague: No offense, but I really don't feel comfortable talking about it, since it is a family matter.

Reiterate excuse: Tell her I'm [work-related errand] and I'll be back at [fill in time].

Define relationship: Well, at least I now know where we stand.

- **Behavior:** Speak with her alone. Remember, you're asking for a favor, so be humble. Keep cool at all times, even if she's pushing for details. Do not, under any circumstances, break down, beg, threaten, or lose your temper. If, after presenting your case, she *still* turns you down, end with a cool and quiet, "Well, at least I now know where we stand with each other," and walk away.

ADAPTATIONS

This script can be modified to:
- Ask a friend to back up a social excuse.

KEY POINTS

- Open with the line, "I need your help." Be as humble and sincere as possible.
- Let her know how long you think you'll be out of the office.
- If she's a friend whom you trust not to gossip, you can tell her why you'll be out, if you choose.
- If you don't trust her not to gossip, tell her you have personal business you need to take care of and leave it at that.
- If she presses, tell her you don't want to talk about it.
- Demonstrate how she can benefit from helping you.
- If she won't help, end with a cold statement of your perception of the relationship.

Asking a Peer to Switch Vacations with You

35.

STRATEGY

In many companies, vacations are spread out so as to minimize their effect on ongoing business. There may come a day when the only way to get the time you want is to switch with a peer who has already reserved that week or weeks. Approach him as soon as you realize you need to switch vacations and be prepared to be flexible. The more notice you give, the better the chance he'll agree, though you may have to alter your ideal plans slightly to make the switch work for both of you. Try to take into account his background and personality. Does the time you're asking for fall on a religious holiday, or is he just religious about spring skiing? If he has chosen to be out of the office when a supervisor or important client is also on vacation, asking him to switch may appear a strategy to outshine him. Having a compelling argument prepared for why you need the time will assuage any such fears. If he can switch but isn't inclined to, be clear that you consider the switch a favor that you'd be pleased to return at a later date. If he still can't or won't capitulate, and if it's truly essential, you can approach your boss with a modified version of this script—just realize that you could be creating an enemy.

TACTICS

- **Attitude:** Depending on the kind of plans he has, you could be asking for a big favor, or it could be no big deal. Be prepared to take no for an answer, but be persistent about wanting the time.
- **Preparation:** Have a compelling list of reasons why you need the time and be ready to juggle days and times with him. Decide if switching with him is the sole or merely the most expeditious option. Have an alternative plan, in case he can't or won't accommodate you.
- **Timing:** The sooner the better. The more notice he has, the better the chance he'll be willing and able to switch.
- **Behavior:** Be positive and upbeat. Enthusiasm for your plans *and* his will help bolster esprit de corps and encourage him to make the switch.

35. Asking a Peer to Switch Vacations with You

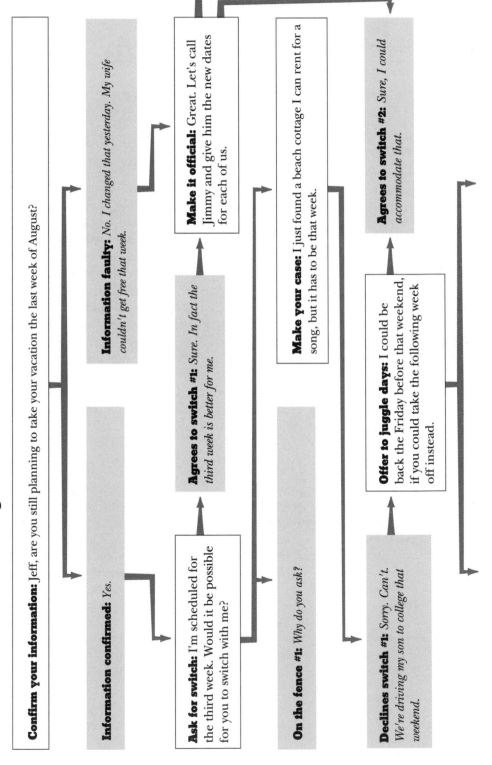

Confirm your information: Jeff, are you still planning to take your vacation the last week of August?

Information confirmed: *Yes.*

Information faulty: *No. I changed that yesterday. My wife couldn't get free that week.*

Ask for switch: I'm scheduled for the third week. Would it be possible for you to switch with me?

Agrees to switch #1: *Sure. In fact the third week is better for me.*

Make it official: Great. Let's call Jimmy and give him the new dates for each of us.

On the fence #1: *Why do you ask?*

Make your case: I just found a beach cottage I can rent for a song, but it has to be that week.

Declines switch #1: *Sorry. Can't. We're driving my son to college that weekend.*

Offer to juggle days: I could be back the Friday before that weekend, if you could take the following week off instead.

Agrees to switch #2: *Sure, I could accommodate that.*

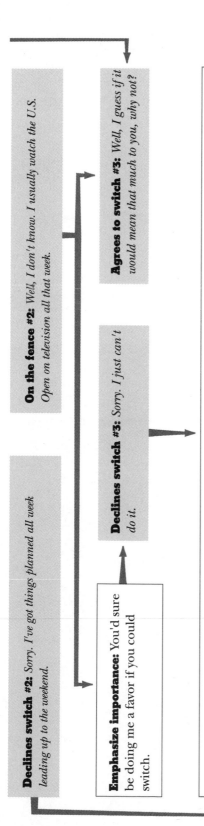

Declines switch #2: *Sorry. I've got things planned all week leading up to the weekend.*

On the fence #2: *Well, I don't know. I usually watch the U.S. Open on television all that week.*

Agrees to switch #3: *Well, I guess if it would mean that much to you, why not?*

Declines switch #3: *Sorry. I just can't do it.*

Emphasize importance: You'd sure be doing me a favor if you could switch.

Thanks anyway: Well, thanks anyway. If your plans change, please let me know.

ADAPTATIONS

This script can be modified to:
- Ask a peer to switch days off.
- Ask a peer to switch assignments with you.
- Ask a supervisor to change your vacation time.

KEY POINTS

- The more notice you give, the better the chance he'll agree.
- Be flexible and prepared to juggle days with him.
- Make your plans sound as compelling and necessary as possible.
- Be polite and positive. You're asking for a favor, but it isn't necessarily a big one.

Asking a Peer for a Date

36.

STRATEGY

Asking anyone on a date is tough, but asking a coworker is especially diffi-cult. If she rejects you, there's nowhere to hide: You'll have to face her every day at work. Your goal should be getting her to accept a social invitation with-out humiliating yourself or destroying your work relationship in the process. The secret to success is breaking this quest down into three parts. If she's new to the company, first approach her as a friendly coworker and ask her to lunch. If she accepts, you'll at least be able to find out whether she's single. If that's all you manage to find out, next invite her out as part of a group and this time find out what her interests are. Use a shared interest as the basis to then finally ask her out alone. If you want to date a longtime coworker, you could casually ask others about her, but make sure whoever you approach can be trusted not to spill the beans or write about your "crush" in the com-pany newsletter. Finally, always have a definite activity and time planned when finally asking someone out on a solo date. "Wanna do something?" isn't just vague, it's boring and desperate, an invitation for instant rejection.

TACTICS

- **Attitude:** Think friendliness and confidence, but not egotism. You're not proposing marriage, so if you're rejected, it should be easy to remain calm and poised.
- **Preparation:** First, determine whether she's available or not. Then find out what she's interested in, either by talking to her yourself or by sub-tly quizzing a third party.
- **Timing:** If she's new to the company and you're suggesting lunch, ask two hours ahead of time. If you already know her, come into work a few minutes early or walk out of the building together so you can speak in private. Don't get so single-minded you forget to sense her mood. If she seems tense or preoccupied, don't push it.
- **Behavior:** You might feel like a nervous wreck on the inside, but your manner must convey confidence and relaxed friendship. Don't stand too close or stare. If she turns you down, be gracious and leave.

36. Asking a Peer for a Date

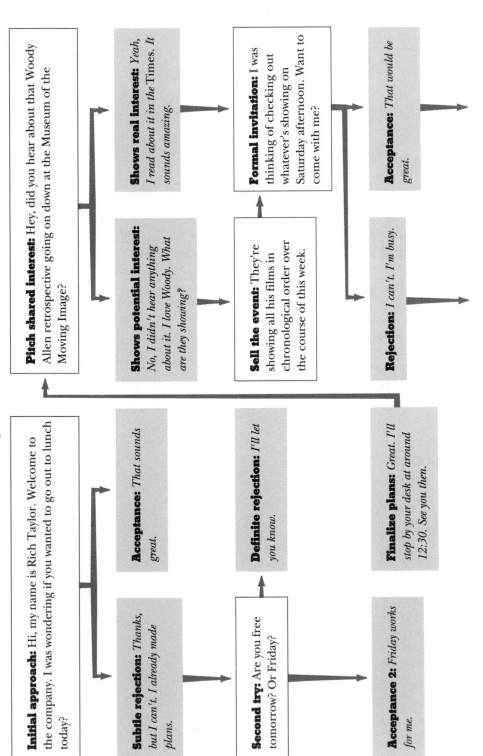

Initial approach: Hi, my name is Rich Taylor. Welcome to the company. I was wondering if you wanted to go out to lunch today?

Acceptance: *That sounds great.*

Subtle rejection: *Thanks, but I can't. I already made plans.*

Second try: Are you free tomorrow? Or Friday?

Definite rejection: *I'll let you know.*

Acceptance 2: *Friday works for me.*

Finalize plans: *Great. I'll stop by your desk at around 12:30. See you then.*

Pitch shared interest: Hey, did you hear about that Woody Allen retrospective going on down at the Museum of the Moving Image?

Shows real interest: *Yeah, I read about it in the Times. It sounds amazing.*

Shows potential interest: *No, I didn't hear anything about it. I love Woody. What are they showing?*

Sell the event: They're showing all his films in chronological order over the course of this week.

Formal invitation: I was thinking of checking out whatever's showing on Saturday afternoon. Want to come with me?

Acceptance: *That would be great.*

Rejection: *I can't. I'm busy.*

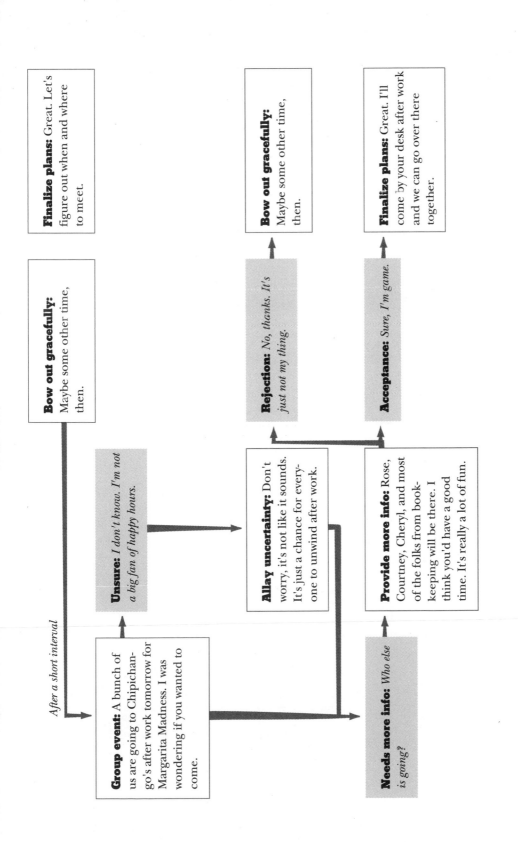

Finalize plans: Great. Let's figure out when and where to meet.

Bow out gracefully: Maybe some other time, then.

Finalize plans: Great. I'll come by your desk after work and we can go over there together.

Bow out gracefully: Maybe some other time, then.

Rejection: *No, thanks. It's just not my thing.*

Acceptance: *Sure, I'm game.*

After a short interval

Unsure: *I don't know. I'm not a big fan of happy hours.*

Allay uncertainty: Don't worry, it's not like it sounds. It's just a chance for everyone to unwind after work.

Provide more info: Rose, Courtney, Cheryl, and most of the folks from book-keeping will be there. I think you'd have a good time. It's really a lot of fun.

Group event: A bunch of us are going to Chipichango's after work tomorrow for Margarita Madness. I was wondering if you wanted to come.

Needs more info: *Who else is going?*

ADAPTATIONS

This script can be modified to:
- Ask an acquaintance out on a date.
- Initiate a friendship with someone you'd like to know better.
- Become friendly with a business contact.

KEY POINTS

- A collegial lunch is the best first step.
- Determine if she's available before going any further.
- An invitation to a group activity can help you glean details.
- Find out whether you share an interest.
- Have a definite activity planned before asking her out.
- Project confidence and friendship throughout.

Deflecting a Peer's Romantic Overtures

37

STRATEGY

If you're single, you'll probably eventually have to deal with romantic overtures from a coworker in whom you have no interest whatsoever. Don't reflexively react with revulsion, horror, embarrassment, or amusement. You'll be seeing this person on the job day in, day out, and you may even have to work closely with him. Your goal should be to deflect his interest in a way that will let you maintain a working relationship. The easiest way to do that is to say you have a steady, serious boyfriend—whether it's true or not. Just be aware that if you lie and he finds out, you'll have made an enemy regardless of how tactfully you originally handled the situation.

TACTICS

- **Attitude:** Be polite, but firm. You can't afford to waffle, since lack of directness may be interpreted as interest, or an opportunity for persuasion. If you respect or pity the flirt, it's OK to indicate you're flattered, just as long as you're still firm in your refusal. If the person making overtures is obnoxious, "polite, but cold" is the formula.
- **Preparation:** Chances are you're going to be blindsided by your coworker/admirer. Still, if you intuitively know someone has a crush on you, try to be ready.
- **Timing:** You have no control over the timing of the initial approach. You do have control over your response, however; you can talk to him there and then and get it over with, or you can try to move the conversation to a different time and place. Awkward as it might be, having the conversation right away is preferable.
- **Behavior:** "Polite, but firm" should be your mantra. Arms crossed will indicate your resoluteness. Try to avoid smiling, frowning, laughing, or smirking.

37. Deflecting a Peer's Romantic Overtures

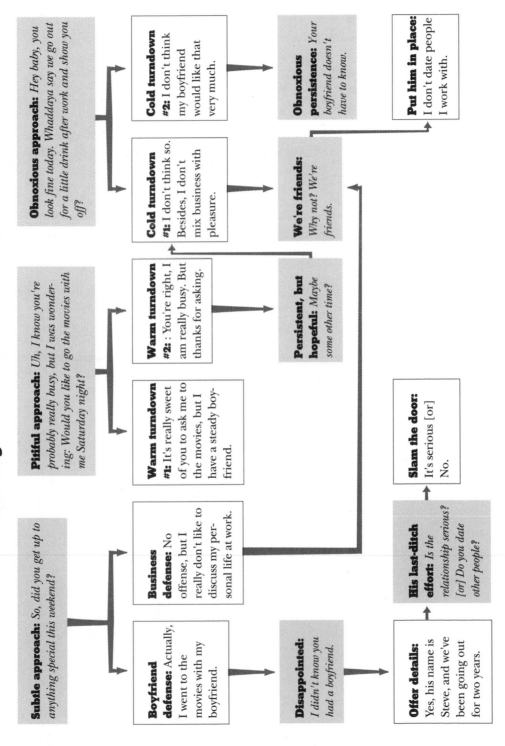

Subtle approach: *So, did you get up to anything special this weekend?*

Boyfriend defense: Actually, I went to the movies with my boyfriend.

Disappointed: *I didn't know you had a boyfriend.*

Offer details: Yes, his name is Steve, and we've been going out for two years.

His last-ditch effort: *Is the relationship serious? [or] Do you date other people?*

Slam the door: It's serious [or] No.

Business defense: No offense, but I really don't like to discuss my personal life at work.

Pitiful approach: *Uh, I know you're probably really busy, but I was wondering: Would you like to go the movies with me Saturday night?*

Warm turndown #1: It's really sweet of you to ask me to the movies, but I have a steady boyfriend.

Warm turndown #2: : You're right, I am really busy. But thanks for asking.

Persistent, but hopeful: *Maybe some other time?*

We're friends: *Why not? We're friends.*

Obnoxious approach: *Hey baby, you look fine today. Whaddaya say we go out for a little drink after work and show you off?*

Cold turndown #1: I don't think so. Besides, I don't mix business with pleasure.

Cold turndown #2: I don't think my boyfriend would like that very much.

Obnoxious persistence: *Your boyfriend doesn't have to know.*

Put him in place: I don't date people I work with.

ADAPTATIONS

This script can be modified to:

- Deflect a friend's, neighbor's, or coworker's religious proselytizing.
- Deflect a friend's, neighbor's, or coworker's political fundraising.

KEY POINTS

- Your goal is to deflect your coworker's interest in a way that allows him to save face and you both to maintain an amicable working relationship.
- No matter what your feelings, be polite, firm, and calm.
- If you have a boyfriend, use him as a means to convey your unavailability.
- If you don't have a boyfriend, but are tempted to lie, think twice. Lies can come back to haunt you.

Telling a Peer Her Job May Be in Danger

38.

STRATEGY

If you've learned, either from a conversation with a supervisor or loose talk around the office, that one of your peers may be terminated, you may want to let her know while there's still a chance for her to save her job. Your goal should be to encourage her to make a candid self-assessment and once she has hit on areas management finds problematic, to suggest simple, effective changes to her work habits. Depending on your relationship and how bad things are, you might also encourage her to start looking for another job. Remember, while some people have a sixth sense for when their tenure at a company is shaky, others don't. If she isn't getting the hint or simply doesn't want your advice, you're better off leaving her be. Avoid being too explicit or naming your source, so as not to endanger your own job.

TACTICS

- **Attitude:** Sure you're doing her a favor, but your primary concern has to be the welfare of the company. Tell her what you think she needs to know to remedy the situation and offer to help in any way you can. But remember, it's up to her to make the changes or move on.
- **Preparation:** Have a couple of her key performance issues in mind and a couple of simple solutions to offer. Realize that personality and corporate culture are sometimes hard to reconcile, so stick to improvements she can realistically accomplish.
- **Timing:** Downtime is the best time to approach your peer as a friend. Arrange to talk outside the office so your conversation will not be overheard, and at the end of the week, so she'll have the weekend to cool down and decide how best to alter her performance or redraft her resume.
- **Behavior:** Be friendly and easygoing, but earnest about the points for improvement you've outlined. You don't need to put the fear of God into her, but you do want her to take you seriously.

38. Telling a Peer Her Job May Be in Danger

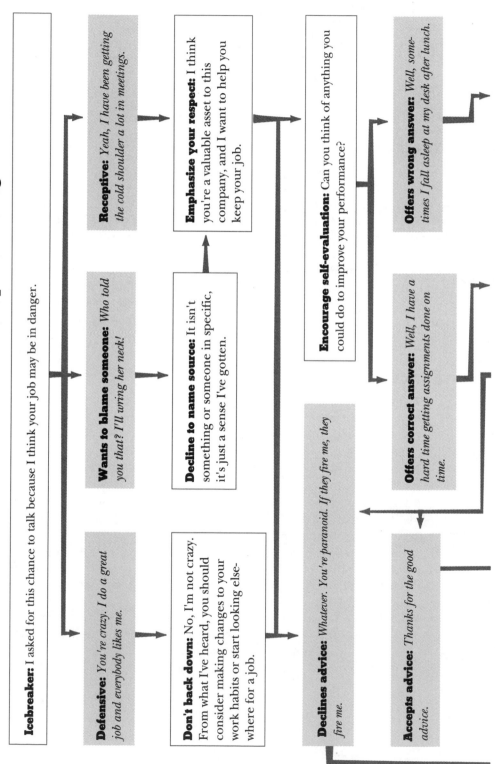

Icebreaker: I asked for this chance to talk because I think your job may be in danger.

Receptive: *Yeah, I have been getting the cold shoulder a lot in meetings.*

Wants to blame someone: *Who told you that? I'll wring her neck!*

Defensive: *You're crazy. I do a great job and everybody likes me.*

Emphasize your respect: I think you're a valuable asset to this company, and I want to help you keep your job.

Decline to name source: It isn't something or someone in specific, it's just a sense I've gotten.

Don't back down: No, I'm not crazy. From what I've heard, you should consider making changes to your work habits or start looking elsewhere for a job.

Encourage self-evaluation: Can you think of anything you could do to improve your performance?

Offers wrong answer: *Well, sometimes I fall asleep at my desk after lunch.*

Offers correct answer: *Well, I have a hard time getting assignments done on time.*

Declines advice: *Whatever. You're paranoid. If they fire me, they fire me.*

Accepts advice: *Thanks for the good advice.*

Focus her on real problem: I didn't realize you did that. That's obviously not a good idea, but I was talking about how you don't complete all your assignments on time.

Denies gravity of problem: *That has only happened a couple of times.*

Offer advice: Why not give yourself an internal deadline in advance of the real deadline so you'll never be late again?

Insist on gravity of problem: I know, but if it continues to happen you could be out of a job.

Accepts problem, but not advice: *I know it's a problem, but I never finished papers on time in college, either. That's just the way I do things.*

End on positive note: Well, I think it's a great company, and I enjoy working with you.

Suggest looking elsewhere: Maybe you should look for a job at a company where deadlines aren't such an important part of the business.

ADAPTATIONS

This script can be modified to:
- Tell a peer to shape up at the request of a supervisor.
- Break bad news so as to encourage action through strategic planning.
- Encourage teamwork to improve a project or department.

KEY POINTS

- Focus on ways she can improve, not what she has already done wrong.
- Decline to name your information source; remain focused on performance, not politics.
- Say what you have to quickly and don't be swayed to say it another time.
- Listen carefully to her self-assessment. If you decide to, you can advocate her side to management and assure them steps are being taken to improve the situation.

Helping a Peer Set More Realistic Goals

39

STRATEGY

Faulting an ambitious coworker isn't justified—unless, of course, in his quest to climb the corporate ladder in record time, he has taken on so much additional work he has let his basic responsibilities slide, leaving the rest of you to pick up the slack. The goal of this lifescript is getting a peer to keep up his basic responsibilities, without damping his enthusiasm for more. Begin by telling him how much you and the rest of the staff admire his dedication and zeal. Then, gently point out how in taking on so many extraneous projects, he hasn't been paying attention to the work at hand, resulting in the rest of you having to cover for him. Ask that he rededicate himself to his basic responsibilities. He will admit he hasn't been paying much attention to his basic work; deny he has let things slide while playing the eager beaver; accuse you of being jealous; or accuse you of being lazy. Whatever his response, you'll need to provide proof you and the rest of the staff have been covering for him while he has been scheming to land a corner office by age twenty-five. If push comes to shove, let him know you're all "mad as hell, and you're not going to take it anymore."

TACTICS

- **Attitude:** Even if his incessant brown-nosing and volunteering for extra work makes you gag, your attitude should be one of appeal. Whatever you do, don't put him down or overtly threaten or undermine him. Remain calm and in control at all times.
- **Preparation:** Talk to your peers and make sure they, too, are feeling resentful of carrying the ball for this guy as he attempts to score brownie points. Once that's confirmed, tell them you plan on having a friendly chat with the gentleman in question, and get their assurance they'll back you up if need be. Concrete examples are crucial.
- **Timing:** Talk to him alone, behind closed doors, preferably after lunch when he should be in a good mood, or when he should be getting down to core tasks.
- **Behavior:** Initially, behave as if you admire the person for working so hard. From there, act as if you're appealing to the person's sense of fairness and rationality. If that fails, make it abundantly clear—without getting nasty—that you and the rest of your cohorts are in no way, shape, or form going to serve as his stepping-stones.

39. Helping a Peer Set More Realistic Goals

Icebreaker: Fox, have you got a minute? I, along with the rest of the department, just wanted you to know that your dedication and enthusiasm lately have really been inspiring. Heck, we're having a hard time keeping up with you! But we've got a slight problem: You've piled so much extra work on your plate that you haven't been paying as much attention to your regular work. The rest of us have been forced to pick up the slack. Maybe you should think about refocusing on your core responsibilities a bit more before taking on anything new.

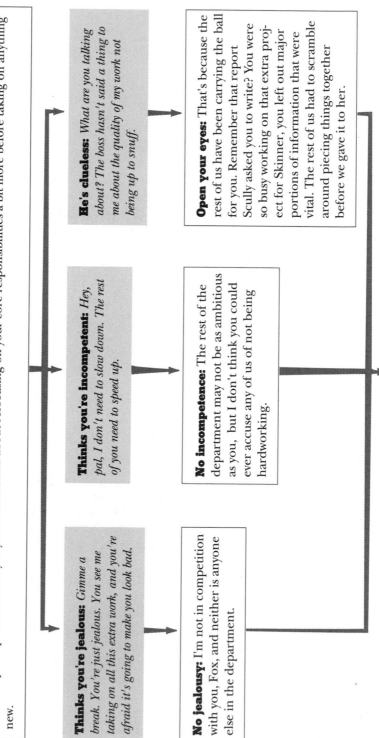

Thinks you're jealous: *Gimme a break. You're just jealous. You see me taking on all this extra work, and you're afraid it's going to make you look bad.*

No jealousy: I'm not in competition with you, Fox, and neither is anyone else in the department.

Thinks you're incompetent: *Hey, pal, I don't need to slow down. The rest of you need to speed up.*

No incompetence: The rest of the department may not be as ambitious as you, but I don't think you could ever accuse any of us of not being hardworking.

He's clueless: *What are you talking about? The boss hasn't said a thing to me about the quality of my work not being up to snuff.*

Open your eyes: That's because the rest of us have been carrying the ball for you. Remember that report Scully asked you to write? You were so busy working on that extra project for Skinner, you left out major portions of information that were vital. The rest of us had to scramble around piecing things together before we gave it to her.

Your pitch: Look, Fox, there's nothing wrong with dreaming big and wanting to get ahead. But that's never going to happen unless you set realistic goals and pay attention to your basic responsibilities. You need to have a solid foundation to rest your reputation on. Without that, you're just building castles in the air that are bound to come crashing down at some point.

Hears threat: *What's this "crashing down" garbage? Are you threatening me?*

Sees the light: *You're right, Alex. I've been so obsessed with getting ahead, I've let my regular work slide. Thanks for pointing it out to me. I'll definitely work on getting my priorities straight from here on in.*

Final response: Of course I'm not threatening you. But none of us appreciate, nor will we continue, picking up the slack caused by your overreaching ambition. [Walk out.]

ADAPTATIONS

This script can be modified to:

- Ask a spouse, partner, child, or sibling to stop pursuing so many extracurricular activities.

KEY POINTS

- Flattery rarely fails. Open the conversation by saying how much you and your colleagues admire his dedication.
- Inform him in delicate terms that his enthusiasm to get ahead has resulted in the rest of you picking up his slack.
- Be able to provide evidence of doing this.
- Ask him to please be fair to the rest of you and refocus on his core responsibilities.
- If this fails, make it clear you and the rest of your peers won't cover for him anymore.
- Remain calm at all times.
- Speak with him alone, preferably after lunch or at a time when he should be focusing on his core responsibilities.

Asking a Peer to Accelerate Her Work

40.

STRATEGY

You truly *can* catch more flies with honey than with vinegar. And when dealing with peers in the workplace, you need honey to spare. Though you and a peer may be handling the bulk of a project's responsibilities, neither of you may be able to control its scheduling. If you need to ask a peer to accelerate her work, you'll need to have empathy and emphasize that circumstances are beyond your control. You need something from your peer—her share of the work, earlier than expected—and nothing works better than good old-fashioned commiseration. Make it clear you're under the same pressures and you'll both need to push harder and work longer hours to meet this new deadline. Resist the temptation to march in and bark orders. Sure you're upset, but being aggressive and demanding will be, well, vinegar. Such an approach might make an overworked and potentially resentful colleague sabotage the project. The desired outcome is the completed project—so don't forget about office harmony. You want to be able to call on this colleague in the future; break the news gently and nonaggressively and make it clear you're a team. Remember, empathize, commiserate, and then get to work.

TACTICS

- **Attitude:** Think humble indignation here. You both need to step up the pace, so express your own frustration and regret, then emphasize the task at hand. Be prepared to handle flak; your colleague might become angry at you for bearing the bad news. Shake it off.
- **Preparation:** Keep the focus on the matter at hand. It would be all too easy to let this slide into an office gripe session, but this is not the time or the place.
- **Timing:** Time is of the essence. As soon as you know of the change, communicate it to your colleague. Don't wait for a "good" time—in this situation, there is none.
- **Behavior:** Remember, you're in this together. Make it clear this change isn't coming from you, but from above. But don't forget the work pace needs to be quickened. Comradeship is key—make it plain you're both invested in this working out.

40. Asking a Peer to Accelerate Her Work

Icebreaker: I just had a meeting with Delano and you're not going to believe this—she told me they need the Melville Project three weeks earlier than scheduled! That only gives us a few days. I'm really sorry to do this to you, Jane, but I'm going to need your drawings right away. Jeez, doesn't management understand we have other projects due? I mean, I've got the Miller Project, the Cereno Project, and now this. I'm going to be camped out here the rest of the week!

Expresses frustration/anger: *What? You've got to be kidding me! I can't just whip out those drawings. This isn't connect the dots. I'm only one person. Doesn't anyone understand that? No, this is totally impossible. There's no way I can get them out by the end of the week.*

Accepts situation: *A few days? No way! I had a feeling about this project. I guess I'd better get going, then. Those drawings are pretty involved. I should call home and tell them I'll be working late tonight and tomorrow....*

Resolution: I owe you, big time, Jane. I know we're really getting squeezed on this one. Let's just get this done. And hey, let me know if you're going on a coffee run.

Restate your position: Jane, come on. I know it's rough, but it's got to get done. If it's any consolation to you, I'll be holed up in my office, too, writing a report that's not even outlined. And remember, if we do really do well on this one, we might get the Dickinson Project.

Accepts situation: *All right. It just makes me angry when orders come down with no understanding of what needs to happen to get them done. I'm sorry I barked at you. I have three other projects I'm working on at the same time. I guess it's nose-to-the-grindstone time, huh?*

Close the conversation: No problem, Jane. I know how it is. We just work here. Anyway, I really appreciate this. We'll have to go out and celebrate when this one is in the can.

Remains angry: *Sure, and make you look good? I bust my butt and let you take the credit. No, thanks. I am an artist, and I will get you the drawings when I feel they are ready.*

State facts: Listen, Jane, I understand your frustration, but there's no reason to get mad at me. I only just found out myself, and I came straight to you. I know it's a pain, but if we don't get it done, we'll be in real danger. If you want to, talk to Delano yourself—she's the one who wants the change. I'm going to my office to get started. Why don't you take a minute to relax, and then come see me. We can work out a schedule for the rest of the week.

ADAPTATIONS

This script can be modified to:

- Tell a friend or family member about a sudden, unavoidable, and inconvenient change in plans.

KEY POINTS

- Soften the blow to your peer by expressing your own frustration at the change in scheduling. Empathy goes a long way here.
- Make sure your colleague is aware these circumstances are beyond your control.
- Be prepared to absorb any anger or frustration from your peer; remember how you felt when you found out about the change. Restate your own frustrations, but stress getting the work done.
- In the event your peer remains angry or becomes critical of you, remain calm, state what you know, and suggest she speak to management.

Asking a Peer to Redo His Work

41.

STRATEGY

Wouldn't it be grand if everything in life went according to plan? Unfortunately, that's rarely the case, especially at work. Projects stamped "finished" can easily land back in the "to be completed" pile because of last-minute changes in circumstance. Maybe some new information has come in that needs to be included in a report, or maybe you just found out the stats that were used need to be replaced pronto. Whatever shift has occurred, the bottom line is that work has to be redone. The goal of this script is getting a peer to redo his work when an unexpected, dramatic shift in circumstances has rendered the work he's already done incomplete or, worse, obsolete. The secret to achieving this is by pointing out to him that *(a)* he really has no choice and *(b)* he's not suffering alone. Everyone is in the same boat.

TACTICS

- **Attitude:** You're appealing for him to do his part. There's no need to resort to threatening, begging, or cajoling. It's OK to demonstrate annoyance—not at him, but over the fact the department has been hit with this at the last minute. But be careful not to let it degenerate into a pity party. Convey a sense of urgency.
- **Preparation:** If you can, find out exactly what your peer needs to redo, as well as when the changes are needed. This will help guarantee speed and efficiency. The last thing in the world you want is to have to go back to him more than once because you were unclear about his role in the revision process. Not only will you look incompetent, but he'll resent you for making his job that much harder.
- **Timing:** Let him know work needs to be redone as soon as possible. It's OK to let him know in front of others since, ostensibly, others in the department—yourself included—are in the same situation.
- **Behavior:** No matter how much work has to redone, do not act hysterical ("Oh, my God, Tyler, you have to redo this NOW or we're all doomed!") or pushy ("Do it now. Do it now. Do it now. Are you doing it now?"). You want to be calm and collected at all times, even if he throws a fit. He may yell. He may cry. He may hurl pencils. It doesn't matter. You are in control, and no matter what, you have to stay that way.

41. Asking a Peer to Redo His Work

Break the bad news: Tyler, got a minute? I hate to be the bearer of bad tidings, but I just found out from sales that some new information has come that has to be included in the quarterly report before we hand it in to the boss. Unfortunately, this means we all have to redo our part of the report, you and me included. Here's what you need to do over. [Give explicit details.]

Wants compensation: *Will we get a bonus?*

No bonus: Look, we don't get paid by the hour, so I doubt we're going to get a bonus. If it helps, consider your bonus the fact that if we do this right, the boss will have continued confidence in our ability to get the job done, and we'll get to keep our jobs.

Apathetic: *No offense, Jon, but it's not my problem. I did what I was asked to do, end of story. I don't care if "new info" has come in.*

Attack apathy: No offense, Tyler, but it is your problem, just like it's my problem and Ann's problem and Dave's problem. Whether we like it or not, we all have to do our part, and that means redoing whatever needs to be redone.

Angry: *Jeez, Jon! I spent three days working on that report! Now you're telling me I have to do the whole thing over?! Forget it!!*

Absorb anger: Look, you have every right to be upset—I'm upset, too! But anger isn't going to make the revisions disappear. Whether we like it or not, we have to do it.

No time: *Look, I don't have time to re-do my part of the report—I'm swamped as it is! They're going to have to hire a temp or a freelancer to make my changes.*

Deflect time problems: News flash, Ty—we're all pressed for time. What we have to do is put other stuff on the back burner for now, and stay late a couple nights this week, maybe even work Saturday. Who knows? Maybe the boss will spring for pizza. We really don't have a choice.

Accepts his fate: *What a nightmare. But I guess we have no choice. I'll put this other stuff aside and start working on it now. Thanks for letting me know.*

ADAPTATIONS

This script can be modified to:

- Ask a family member or friend to redo a chore or a task.

KEY POINTS

- Make it clear from the outset that he's not the only one who has to redo his work; others in the department have to as well.
- Know exactly what it is he needs to redo and by when it needs to be done.
- As soon as you're aware he needs to redo work, tell him.
- Stay calm at all times when dealing with him, even if he pitches a fit.
- Convey a sense of urgency without coming across as hysterical or pushy.

NOTES

NOTES

NOTES

NOTES

NOTES

NOTES